WILD WITH CHILD

ADVENTURES OF FAMILIES IN THE GREAT OUTDOORS

WILD WITH CHILD

ADVENTURES OF FAMILIES
IN THE GREAT OUTDOORS

Edited by

JENNIFER BOVÉ

SOLAS HOUSE, INC.

PALO ALTO

Cover design and front cover photography: Kimberly Nelson
Interior layout: Cynthia Lamb, using the font Bembo
Back cover author photo: Chris Bové
Production Director: Christy Quinto

Distributed by: Publishers Group West, 1700 Fourth Street, Berkeley,
California 94710.

Library of Congress Cataloguing-in-Publication Data

Wild with child : adventures of families in the great outdoors / edited by
Jennifer Bové.
    p. cm.
 Includes bibliographical references.
 ISBN 978-1-932361-87-2 (pbk.)
 1. Family recreation. 2. Outdoor recreation. 3. Parent and child.
I. Bové, Jennifer, 1973-
 GV182.8.W55 2010
 790.1'91--dc22

2010015654

First Edition
Printed in the United States
10 9 8 7 6 5 4 3 2 1

Table of Contents

Foreword
Into the Wild

MARK JENKINS

Teal is frying salami in our snowcave, as is the tradition, the primal aroma curling through the small, icy enclosure. Fried salami is her "invention." Three or four years ago, in another snowcave, she inexplicably wanted bacon for breakfast and being a good dad I'd packed only oatmeal.

"Oatmeal tastes like cardboard," she said, whereupon she crawled out of her sleeping bag, dug through the food, fished out a package of lunch salami and insisted I teach her how to light the little stove. She was seven years old and already a confirmed vegetarian, *except* during camping trips. We've had fried salami for breakfast ever since.

Teal, eleven, and her sister Addi, thirteen, have been winter camping since they were toddlers. And not just with me; Sue, my wife, has taken them on numerous all-girl, no-boys-allowed winter excursions. Having done two expeditions a year for a quarter century—the Andes to the Arctic, the Himalayas to the Hindu Kush, making a living from writing about these journeys—I want them to experience the joy of becoming competent campers. Every spring, when the days are long and warm and pleasantly unwinterlike, we ski up into the Rockies, burrow out a snowcave, and camp. There is no agenda. Once we spent the better part of a brilliantly sunny day following marmot tracks around in the snow. Another time we played cards for hours—Rummy, Speed, McGivers, Go Fish—while an unexpected blizzard howled above us.

Here's a fact seemingly forgotten in our wired-wimpy-shopping-mall world: kids are natural little outdoor people. It is we, the adults, that turn them into indoor people. If you don't get off your computer, why should they?

Being a parent (read: know-it-all) it has taken my daughters their entire lives to teach me the five basic tricks to taking kids into the wild.

One: get organized. If it takes you more than three hours to get out the door your kids will be moaning, the initial passion will have passed, and you'll never go. Both my girls have an outdoor dresser in the basement stuffed with their own gear—backpack, sleeping bag, headlamp, survival kit, etc. Divide duties. One adult do the food, one do the camping gear, kids do their own personal accoutrement, clothes to compass (Dad's rule in our household: only one stuffed animal per girl).

Two: give your kids responsibility. Once outside, let them lead, who cares if you get lost; it might be the best trip you ever have. Let them choose where to pitch the tent and figure out how to put it up. Let them cook, what's a singed finger or two? Stop telling them what to do. If they want to wear shorts and get eaten alive by mosquitoes, let 'em. Far as I can tell, one of the biggest mistakes we're making in our urban existence is not letting kids make mistakes. The great outdoors is a fine place to give them the chance to make meaningful decisions, screw up, re-evaluate.

Three: stop worrying about whether they can handle it. You want the truth? Your kid is hardier than you are. I remember Addi, at age eight, making three portages with packs better than half her weight on a weeklong Boundary Waters canoe trip. Why? Because Sue explained that the best swimming hole on the planet was at the next lake. And, because we stopped and spent the rest of the afternoon there, it was. Kids are tough. Ever witness a child take a bad digger on the playground? Without adults around, he'll get up, consider crying, but go back to playing instead.

(One caveat: there are trips I will not take children on, namely all those in which there are too many dangers out of my control. Class III or better whitewater, high altitude peaks, high avalanche-prone terrain, that sort of thing. You can't control nature, but you can choose your wilderness wisely.)

Four: fun. Forget your boring, goal-oriented adult approach. Kids just wanna have fun. So let them. No death marches to reach the next camp. Get sidetracked. "Waste" an hour with your nose two inches from a mountain tarn watching tadpoles. Catch a few. Play games. My girls love treasure hunts. I'll set up a little course where they have to take compass bearings to each new clue. Ever notice that when a child is having fun, she doesn't get cold or hungry or tired? The moment the fun stops, the whining starts.

A most important corollary to fun, is friends. One kid in the mountains with two adults is disaster. Let them bring a friend or two, you'll thank God you did.

Finally, five: let them be wild. Gleefully throw out the rules we all live by in civilized society. I distinctly remember a marshmallow-roasting contest that got totally out-of-hand and both girls ended up with gooey smears of blackened marshmallow in their hair. (Kids adore dirt. Besides, cleanliness is a modern fetish. If they don't get dirty camping, you're doing something wrong.) Or the time we played chase around a small set of cliffs and pretty soon they were jumping off rocks ten feet high. Just short of injury, let 'em go. Hell, if you can't go wild in the wilds, where can you?

Kids are natural born adventurers. Inside every one of them is Huck Finn, just itching to get outside. Open the door and follow them out.

Formerly "The Hard Way" columnist for Outside *magazine, Mark Jenkins is currently a field staff writer for* National Geographic Magazine. *His work has appeared in* The Atlantic Monthly, National Geographic, GQ, Playboy, Men's Health, *and dozens of other publications. His books are:* Off the Map, To Timbuktu, The Hard Way, *and* A Man's Life. *Mark also contributed "The Snowcave" and "From the Mouths of Babes" to this collection.*

Introduction

Bright sky and towering treetops reflected in the stormy blue of my baby boy's eyes, and I wondered how the world looked to him. To me, it was sublime: my son cradled on my lap and miles of forest surrounding us in every direction. At four days old, there's no way I would have exposed him to any public setting where people would sneeze, cough, and reach out to touch him. But even as fresh as he was, I felt entirely comfortable having him there, amid that sacred ground, where giant firs and clear river water offered respite on a hot July day, and ripe berries dotted lush green bushes like jewels.

As I wrapped Sam in his soft cloth sling and secured him against my chest, I could hear my daughters' chattering and laughter as they bobbed through the brush with their grandmother. Big Daddy was already off filling his bucket in earnest, hoping to bring home gallons of huckleberries for the freezer and determined to do it all on his own if he had to. For a moment, I could only stand still and breathe it in, the peace of the place and my people. Huckleberry picking, we've found, soothes some feral part of this family that paces its cage as we go through the motions of "normal" life. The simple act of wandering and harvesting food directly from its source reconciles us with our wild roots. The kids can scramble around for hours, playing or picking and nibbling with abandon, and at the end of the day they're purple-stained forest critters, calm and unburdened, with just enough energy left to catch a quick river swim before exhaustion drags them down for naps. On those days, the calluses of more civilized obligations are stripped away, and our sensitivity of spirit is renewed.

I doubt our son will ever have any conscious remembrance of his fourth day, nursing amid a halo of huckleberries or dipping his tiny toes into the glacial spill of the Cle Elum River, but I know that these things are part of who he is, just as they are a part of his father, his sisters, and me. And I hope that by sowing our kids in wild country, they will internalize not only a love for nature but also the instinct to seek comfort in its fold. After all, it is their source, their mother before me.

People who love the wilderness, who get out into it and get dirty and sweaty and feel they are better for it, are drawn to it for life. It isn't a whim that fades with age or evolves into a placid acceptance of interior spaces. It's a blessing, and maybe a little bit of a curse, because it takes hold of you when you've been inside too long and yanks you by the gut, burns in your veins till you give in and get outside. If you shun it, you shun the very essence of who you are.

But even the intrepid sometimes succumb to the *other* undeniable force of nature: reproduction. Whether it's the biological clock nipping at our heels, hankering, or happenstance, it befalls a good number of us. It happened to me, despite an almost manic resolution that it never would, and I admittedly had a hard time getting used to the idea. After the ready-or-not blow of finding out I was pregnant, I was awfully glad I had nine months to ruminate about *me the outdoorswoman* coming to grips with *me the parent*. Much to my bewilderment, those infamous nesting hormones kept compelling me toward the vacuum cleaner on perfectly sunny November days. And I had to shake my head once in a while to rid it of the wrestling match between soft, cuddly baby buntings and boots caked in mountain mud. How could I have both?

I don't think I really understood the silliness of my internal struggle until after my first child was born, at which point I realized that she had no inherent interest in keeping me locked up indoors. This curious little newborn person was happy to be bundled up in a cozy wrap and packed right out into a cold winter day, curling quietly against my body as I walked wherever I wanted, until *my* toes complained of cold inside my beloved boots. Back home, when I'd unwrap her, she'd look up at me calmly with pink cheeks to show for our outing, and I knew that we were going to get along just fine.

When I set out to gather stories for *Wild with Child*, I was excited to meet so many other men and women like me who are bound by a mutual rope as they rappel the rock face of parenthood. In our own ways, we are reshaping the ancestral art of raising outdoor children because we enjoy being out there so much ourselves. We want to teach our offspring about nature and our own wild tendencies, and we enjoy learning from the fresh, bright-eyed perspectives of these small savants. But many of us also felt some degree of trepidation when faced with the prospect of modifying our lifestyles to include youngsters. Would we have to become so slow and safe that heading out into rugged country wouldn't even be worth the effort? The answer comes back to the simple fact that the yen for wilderness will not be ignored. Like I said, no matter how many doors you close, it finds you and beckons you back. So, even though few aspects of parenting are easy—and getting outdoors is certainly no exception—there just isn't any other option.

Whether just beginning the course or looking back at the trail they've taken, the writers in this book aren't willing to accept Disneyland as the final frontier. Even the most civilized among them insist that their children grow up feeling grass between their toes and sun on their skin. It is a healthy heritage; it gives kids a steady set of bearings, makes them strong. Through trial and error, these parents have figured out that kids will rise to challenges with valor and vigor, and will thrive on time spent out of the house. The bottom line: there just isn't any sense in staying cooped up inside once you've got nestlings in tow.

On the trek you're about to take through this book, you'll explore the diverse terrain of wild parenting, experiencing joys, trials, and triumphs along the way. You may want to bundle up, though, before you strike out into the Rocky Mountains with Mark Jenkins, whose idea of quality kid time is camping in a snow cave. Along for the ride with Karen Fisher and family, you'll discover for better or worse that off-road family expeditions don't always turn out as planned. You'll also share Leslie Leyland Fields' deep gratitude as her brood safely migrates to an Alaskan island by bush plane, and remember that a bonding experience is worth a bit of risk when you take to the river with Fred Bahnson and his boy. Maleesha Speer confides her personal evolution as she awakens to the wonder of her unborn child in bear country; Diane Selkirk's daughter will wrap you around her little finger, convincing you that the delight is in the details; and Ana Rasmussen will lead you up the trunk of a giant pine tree in search of a sense of connection with her nearly grown son.

That, my friends, is just a taste of the adventures waiting in *Wild with Child*. If I gave it all away now, I'd spoil the fun. Suffice to say that if you're an active outdoor mom or dad, you'll find acres of common ground among these parents. On the other hand, if you're struggling with the idea of leading your kids beyond the front door, you can certainly save yourself some scrapes and bruises by experiencing how others have done it. You're sure to laugh, shudder, shake your head, and sigh—and by the time you've finished the book, you'll feel as if the authors are old friends, even family. Adventure has a way of bringing people together—sometimes the tougher the experience, the tighter the bond. So be brave, shoulder your pack, and take hold of your child's hand. There are wonders waiting and memories to be made. And I'll bet you a bunch of batteries and matches and chocolate bars that you'll agree when I tell you that it's all worth it in the end.

—JENNIFER BOVÉ
Calico Rock, Arkansas

BETSY KEPES

Uphill Infinity and the Chocolate Chip Cookies

*When the trail gets tough, there's nothing like cookies
to pull you through.*

IN MY HEAD I AM A CARTOON WOMAN. MY TWO-DIMENSIONAL silhouette has a long braid and carries a toddler in a backpack. Ahead is a steeply uptilted line with an arrow that says "Infinity." This then is misery, hiking uphill forever with an active two-year-old on my back.

"Mom, tell me another story!" Jay jumps up and down in anticipation and the straps of his backpack dig into my shoulders. He seems to have gained ten pounds since breakfast.

"Jay, I'm carrying you up a big mountain and I'm too tired to tell more stories. Why don't you play with your Matchbox truck?" I pull a miniature red pickup truck out of the voluminous fanny pack that I've reversed into a belly bag. A small hand appears at my shoulder to receive the toy and, for the moment, Jay's bouncing stops.

It's been fifteen years since I've hiked this trail in the Selway-Bitterroot Wilderness and in that time it's grown longer and steeper. The switchbacks curve up and up, biting into the massive mountainside above us. Somewhere up ahead is Freeman Ridge, but it will be hours yet before we get there.

*

This wilderness traverse had seemed like a great idea when Tom and I and the boys were still in our fire lookout tower, packing up for the end of the season. We needed to get to the Bitterroot Valley and rather than finding a ride we'd begin on the Selway River in Idaho and hike the fifty-seven miles to the other side of the wilderness in Montana. It would be our grand finale family trip after a summer of shorter weekend hikes. Lee, who had just turned ten, was an enthusiastic hiker with strong legs and it would be wonderful to show him the area where Tom and I had worked on a trail crew years before he was born. Little Jay had recently discovered the joys of small cars and trucks and he would love playing on the white sand beaches along the Selway.

Yet even in the midst of my excitement over the trip I felt a bit of misgiving. We had only four days to do the traverse and because we had finished our work for the Forest Service, we'd have to turn in our portable two-way radio. We'd be backpacking long distances through one of the wildest places in the Lower 48 with a ten-year-old, a two-year-old, and absolutely no way to call for help. "We'll be careful," I assured myself as I stood in our airy lookout house and baked an enormous batch of cookies, using the last of our margarine, sugar, and chocolate chips.

"Ouch! Jay, don't pull my hair." Jay yanks his tiny pickup truck from my head, pulling my hair again. He's been driving the truck up and down my back and shoulders and narrating his play with nonstop verbal pretend. Jay, who didn't say a word until age two, is now, six months later, a loquacious conversationalist. As much as I am pleased he's overcome his early reluctance to talk, I wish he'd learn to keep a few thoughts to himself. After all, his mouth is right behind my ears.

"Tell a story! Tell a story, *please*, Mom!"

Do I have any stories left in me? This is the third day of our trip and to keep Jay entertained I've been talking until I'm hoarse. We've stayed on schedule though, hiking in two days the twenty-six miles along the spectacular Selway River trail to the interior Moose Creek Ranger Station. Tom carries an enormous Kelty frame pack stuffed with most of our camping gear and food. Lee bounces along under a kids' pack heavy with cookies and other sweets, a portable snack bar. He is proud to be carrying the most delicious portion of our food for the trip.

"Jay, stop that!" I swing around, as if somehow my pack won't go with me. "You do *not* pinch people! No stories for boys who pinch."

My anger propels me up the next stretch of trail, and Jay is quiet. The silence that I had wanted so desperately now makes me feel uneasy. I am teaching my son to hate backpacking. He'll never want to take a wilderness journey again.

"Oh, Jay, look!" Ahead of us a dark fuzzy animal sits in the trail, a black bear cub. Confused, it whines softly then climbs a small tree.

I look around for its mother while slowly stepping past the tree, turning so Jay can have a good look at the cub. I don't take a full breath until we're a quarter-mile up the trail. Mama Bear will know now that I don't intend to harm her offspring.

Jay hasn't said anything since the pinching incident. Now he reaches forward, pats my cheek, and says in his gravelly little boy voice, "This is really fun, Mom."

Around the next corner we find Tom and Lee taking a break. Lee lies on his back in the middle of the trail, his arm draped across his forehead.

"Is Lee sleeping?" Jay asks, pushing himself up on my shoulders to get a better look.

"No. He's just being dramatic," Tom answers and I can hear the frustration in his voice. I bet I can persuade him to swap sons. "He thinks this mountain is too tall."

"I am *so* tired." Lee sits up quickly. "Can we have our cookies now?"

I look at my watch—9 A.M. Before dawn we left the porch of the empty ranger's cabin at Moose Creek and shuffled carefully along the trail in the dark, trying to avoid tripping on roots and rocks. Jay snuggled against my back, his body warm in a thick wool poncho. After the new pink of dawn we sat on an open slope to eat breakfast and said goodbye to the Selway River far below us. This is our most ambitious day of backpacking—a 5,000-foot climb to the ridge, then eight more miles to our destination, Indian Lake. If we don't keep moving we'll never make it by dark.

"Put me down, Mom. I want to play with Lee."

"O.K., but this is a *short* stop, you two." I feel like an evil prison warden, reluctantly doling out a few minutes of recreation time.

After a couple of greasy chocolate chip cookies the boys are running around on the trail, completely revived. Tom and I sit watching and resting. I need this break too, but I glance at my watch nervously. We have so many more miles to go.

I carry Tom's big pack on the next section of trail. It is heavier than my pack with Jay but it doesn't squirm or talk. It's too big for me and I have to walk with my hands cupped around the bottom of the frame, heaving the pack up now and then so the hip belt doesn't sink down to my thighs. Still, it doesn't yell in my ear, pinch me, or tangle trucks in my hair.

By lunchtime we've made it almost to the top of the ridge and in the afternoon we hike long miles through a recent burn where jagged blackened tree trunks and a vigorous growth of weeds have replaced the forests we remembered. Jay listens carefully to Tom's stories while Lee and I, walking ahead and out of earshot, have our own, more sophisticated, conversation.

After miles and miles of ridge walking past spindly sub-alpine fir and lumpy meadows of beargrass, we arrive at the site of the old Freeman Lookout. Lee and I explore the ruins, poking through melted window glass, copper wire, rusty nails, and a metal box that once held the phone equipment look-outs used before radios. Tom sits perched on a rock, carefully leaning the kid carrier pack against a boulder, trying not to disturb Jay from his afternoon nap, the only time of day that our toddler is quiet.

We didn't have much of a fire season on our lookout. Whenever we saw thunderstorms, they fizzled out before they reached our district. But now, as we leave the old lookout site we see an active storm cell approaching and this one doesn't dissipate. From the dark swirl of cloud, lightning flashes and the thunder is so loud it hurts my ears. I flinch as down-strikes start new fires less than a mile away from us; we can see burning trees on a nearby ridge. We *must* get off this exposed section of trail.

I begin an awkward jog, the giant pack bending me forward at the waist. "Lee! Tom! Move as fast as you can but don't walk together!" In my panicked reasoning it seems that if we space ourselves along the trail, some of us will survive a direct hit. I don't want to follow that thought out to its conclusion— if Tom or I are struck we have no one left to run for help, no radio, no phone and it's a two-day walk to the nearest road.

My heart is racing and it feels as if pure adrenaline is flowing in my veins.

Lee stops and I almost run into him. He turns around with a wide grin and says, "Wow, look at that cloud! Doesn't it look like a tornado?"

I have to admit that it does, though my reaction isn't as gleeful. "Keep moving, Lee! Keep moving!"

Just what we need, central Idaho's first mountain tornado. Fortunately it is only a trick of the late afternoon light. Unfortunately, the not-a-tornado cloud is filled with cold rain. It pulses down in sheets of water. We have only a few miles to go to get to Indian Lake so we push on, heads down. When we scramble off the ridge I remind myself to be grateful—we made it off the ridge with no one electrocuted—but as the rain runs down my neck it is difficult to be thankful for much.

The last couple of miles are of the infinity type, an endless up and down on muddy trail through the soggy grasslands of Horsefly Meadows and up and over a small ridge. My legs are so tired they are quivering with fatigue. Amazingly, Jay keeps on with his nap, oblivious to the deafening thunder and icy rain, with his poncho and raincoat draped over his relaxed body. And Lee actually picks up his pace, a small sturdy workhorse heading for the barn.

After fourteen hours on the trail, we hike into the Indian Lake basin. As we arrive Jay wakes up and realizes he is wet and cold and hungry and lets loose with giant sobs. Tom tries to comfort him while we look around for a campsite. In a hurry, we make do with a bumpy hollow in a landscape of burned trees. My hands are shaking from cold, exhaustion, and worry as I thud my giant backpack against a tree and stretch my aching shoulders.

"Cookies, Lee. We need the cookies."

The four of us sit on a log, soaked and shivering, each of us gobbling a big chocolate chip cookie. I can almost feel the sugar calories flowing into my bloodstream.

"O.K." I jump up off the log. "Lee, strip off all your wet clothes, put on long johns, wool hat, everything warm left in your pack. Tom, I'll get Jay dry if you get the tent up."

From the bottom of our packs we pull out our emergency bags of clothes, clothes we haven't needed on our other, warmer and drier, summer trips. Lee, his wet hair plastered over his eyes, holds his bag like a precious treasure and muses, "Now I see why you made me carry this around all summer!"

In the last bit of daylight we crawl into the tent and smile at the luxury of warm, dry sleeping bags. Jay, who loves our nylon playroom, bounces around, giggling and climbing up the mountains made by our bent knees. Lee wants to hear more of our read-aloud but, exhausted by the long day, he falls asleep before Tom finishes the first page.

It takes longer for Jay to settle down. I let him draw in my journal and Tom plays Hide-and-Seek with Jay's little stuffed monkey, a wise simian who speaks in a high squeaky voice and who suggests numerous times that Jay snuggle quietly into his spot in the sleeping bag.

Finally Jay closes his eyes. Tom is asleep beside him, the little monkey still held in his hand. I turn off my headlamp and through the tent screen I can see stars. For our last full day on the trail we'll have clear weather. The route will be long, but not as uphill. No doubt we'll have difficult moments, but we'll also find time to go for a swim in Wahoo Creek and admire the beauty of this rugged country. The boys will make sure we stop for enough breaks, and tucked in Lee's pack is one last bag of cookies.

I pull the sleeping bag up around Jay's small shoulders, inhale a slow and full breath, and let it out in a long, satisfied sigh.

Betsy Kepes lives in the northern Adirondack Mountains of New York during the school year and works as a piano teacher and freelance writer. In the summer she and her family migrate to Idaho where they become a wilderness trail crew and forest fire lookouts. In her spare moments she runs marathons, writes children's books, and does historical research and re-enactments.

FRED BAHNSON

✳

The Tender Groin
of the Land

What's a little risk when you're wading to Paradise?

THE TUCKASEGEE, WALKING UPRIVER IN THE RAIN, MY SON riding piggyback.

We tried to get to Paradise. The swimming hole, Paradise. That's what the Clarke family has called it since the twenties, and the name is apt. A little Shangri-La on the Blue Ridge. On a clear July afternoon there's no better place to be than sprawled out at the bend in the river below Third Falls, an eighty-foot drop that echoes through the canyon's mouth, speaking a word of wildness. At Paradise, there's so much to see that you never think of leaving.

Elizabeth and I went to Paradise two years before on our honeymoon; now we wanted to take our nine-month-old son Carsten. But the rain stopped us. When we got to the crossing below Second Falls the river was too high. Paradise would have to wait. We turned back toward the cabin, where we'd settle on the back porch and enjoy the more profane pleasures of steak and Shiraz, watch lightning bugs punctuate the sentence of a long summer evening.

We climbed back upriver the way we'd descended, past the rambling slide of Second Falls, then the sudden hard drop of

First Falls, where Elizabeth's Uncle Bobo drowned, all this time the rain pounding hard. When we passed First Falls it let up some, and we stopped to rest before the final stretch of flat river that would take us back to the cabin. It was nearly 7 P.M. These July evenings were long, but darkness was coming soon.

It was that last bit of light falling on the river, I think, that gave rise to my vision.

New sounds replaced the rain—crickets, frogs, water dripping off tree leaves onto the forest floor. The Tuckasegee slid toward the three falls in a languid torpor, as if ignorant of the awaiting plunge. While I watched, the air became as blue as the water itself, a dusky light cutting through hemlock and pine at such an oblique angle that the evening seemed to lie down on the river in great billowing sheets, until finally you couldn't tell where air ended and water began. I wanted to wade out into this watery half-dark, immerse myself in the gloaming.

Since the twenties the Tuckasegee headwaters and environs have been the vacation spot for my wife's family. The Clarkes owned the land just below Panthertown, near the headwaters, but they claimed the entire watershed as if it were theirs, calling it simply Tuckasegee (Tucka-*see*-gee). From the beginning of our courtship Elizabeth and I spent weekends here. I began to explore the place, wanting to know it as well as I did my native Gallatin Valley in southwest Montana. On my rambles I had walked this trail beside the river many times, going back and forth between the cabin and the three falls downstream. I'd forded the Tuckasegee without a thought; swam in its plunge-pools, jumped off its cliffs, fanned lizard-like on its sandy banks. I knew the river held power; but I thought of that power in terms of its waterfalls, its big drops, its dangerous rapids.

Here, at rest, the river was altogether different. Along this calm stretch I saw working the subtle interplay of power and finesse, the strength inherent in all things quiet and still. I wanted to enter this power. And in some pre-linguistic way, I wanted my son to enter it, too.

"I want to take Carsten upriver," I told Elizabeth.

She looked at me, paused, then said, "What do you mean *upriver*? We've been hiking upriver since below Second Falls."

"No, no" I said, spreading my arms over the water. "I mean *in* it. I want to walk *in* the river."

Elizabeth sucked in her cheeks. Carsten was only nine months old. Carrying him in a backpack upriver, *in* the water—I could see the flashing lights blink on inside the Maternal Warning System.

"Well," she said, and looked out over the river. Perhaps she began to see there a glimpse of what I saw, felt the pull of water. "It *is* pretty calm the rest of the way back. Though it's going to take you a while. You know it'll be dark soon." She wasn't saying no, wasn't saying yes. She wanted me to see the foolhardiness of my proposition.

"It's only seven," I said. "We'll be at the cabin in twenty minutes."

Her teeth pulled at her lower lip. "O.K." Then, as an afterthought: "But why do you want to walk upriver?"

My eyes tracked the course we'd take until the Tuckasegee disappeared around a bend. The river was like a forgotten road you might find wandering the countryside, one that leads to a darkened wood in the distance.

There's a blessing waiting for us. This is what my father would say before setting out on one of our climbing adventures. And there would be. Sometimes the blessing would be a marmot whistling from a talus slope in the Tetons; or the blessing would be a serendipitous moment, like reading the name of a famous mountaineer in a summit register; or the rare oddity, like the time we were hiking at the base of the Matterhorn and found protruding from the glacier a human foot. On the foot was a late-1930's hob-nailed *klettershoe,* leather laces snugged tight around the ankle bones.

Blessings turned up everywhere if you paid attention.

"If a child is to keep alive his inborn sense of wonder," Rachel Carson wrote, "he needs the companionship of at least one adult who can share it, rediscovering with him the joy, excitement, and mystery of the world we live in." To Carson's maxim I'd add: adults need the companionship of at least one child. It's children that keep us bound to this mysterious world. We're too prone to abstraction without them. We adults shouldn't be allowed to wander through this life without a child holding our hand. Or riding on our back.

Though a shrug was all I could muster at the time, the answer to Elizabeth's question was simple. Our small purpose, my son and I, walking upriver along the Tuckasegee, was this: to help each other keep alive our sense of wonder.

To pay attention. To find the blessing.

Elizabeth pays attention. Earlier, on our way down to Paradise, she pointed out flora on the trail: Jack-in-the-Pulpit, Indian Cucumber, Punk Tatum, Dog Hobble, and Little Brown Jug, the last one a fancy name for wild ginger root.

Thousands of white lights lit up the dark woods. Elizabeth picked one, showing me the stickiness on the rhododendron flower's stem. We grabbed handfuls and pasted them on each others' noses and foreheads. We put a pair on Carsten's ears. Then, with mock solemnity, we set off up the trail like proud forest people.

The path was root-strewn and wet. Above us, rhododendrons, Carolina hemlocks, and Frasier firs formed a canopy. Sunlight never reached the ground, which was springy and black like chocolate sponge cake. A shimmering-wet mixture, like Thoreau's "quaking sphagnum." Each step released the dank scent of moss, dead leaves, and the sweet skunkiness of galax, that ubiquitous odor Elizabeth calls "the smell of Tuckasegee." Satisfying smells, all of them, and strangely comforting. Here in this place that never dries out the entire forest floor along the river seemed to sway and hum with a secret, pulsing life. All this time the river ran beside us along the trail, waiting to dole out its store of mysteries like those a sage bestows upon the weary pilgrims who come seeking.

When Elizabeth left us I walked down the bank and dipped a foot in the water. So clear, so cold—both rare qualities for North Carolina rivers in late July. The water felt as frigid as the snow-fed Montana rivers of my boyhood. We were only a few miles from Panthertown, the Tuckasegee's source, where mountain springs arose from deep in the earth, rushed downhill in blind search of other streams, all making their way toward equilibrium and repose.

I remembered a line from James Agee I'd read that morning, sitting on the cabin's back porch waiting for the rain to quit: "Eternal, lithe, fingering, chiseling, searching out the tender groin of the land." Agee was describing the Mississippi, but his words made me think of the Tuckasegee. *Life, fecundity, regeneration*: these things the river seeks. And creates.

How intricate and beautiful was the river, and how glad I was for bringing my son here. Together we looked up at the forest of arms, hands, fingers, all reaching over our heads to hold the dying light.

The air was a taut string—no, thousands of strings, all plucked in unison: insects thrummed, skimmed, and buzzed in a symphony of wings. Into this aerial orchestra dragonflies dove, plucking away the musicians one by one. All this rowdiness must have pleased Carsten. Each time a pair of wings dipped close, he dug his bare toes into my back and squealed.

The water was clear as breath, as clean a river as I'd seen in North Carolina. Through its translucence hundreds of intricate sand ridges shimmered along the river bottom. Like a miniature desert. I put my face close to the water to look and watched as sand grains swirled, blown by the current's wind into a ridge-and-valley line of dunes so tiny that my sandaled footprint spanned a dozen.

This Tuckasegee of ours could easily have been a quiet section of the Gallatin, or Madison, or Jefferson—Montana rivers I'd known as a child. There on those rivers my brother, Carsten's namesake, and I would scour the shallows for crawfish. When we caught five or six we'd boil them for lunch in a halved Coors Light can filled with river water. Mom would offer us bologna sandwiches, but we refused them. We preferred river meat. I can still taste its swampy flavor. Like undercooked shrimp wrapped in seaweed.

Gallatin. Madison. Jefferson. Even today, when I hear those names I think not of presidents but of rivers. Every spring snowmelt from three mountain ranges—the Spanish Peaks, the Bridgers, and the Tobacco Roots—rushes into those three rivers, pushing them toward their meeting point where they become the Missouri. *Perichoresis* is how the early church fathers described the Trinity—an interpenetration of the three persons, an eternal dance between Father, Son, and Holy Ghost. That's how I think of the Missouri headwaters: an interplay of triune movement, a three-in-one torrent of cold unity.

*

Walking up the river, which varied between knee-deep and waist deep, was an exercise in patience. It slowed us down. We had more time to engage, to notice something as simple and lovely as a rhododendron flower reflected on the water. Water skippers skimmed over the flower's reflection like dozens of six-bristle brushes painting rhodo-white onto a palate of river-blue. "Look," I said, bending down to the water so Carsten could see, and he looked, serious with intent, as if the flower's opaque image was a mysterious puzzle to be solved.

The Tuckasegee was getting deeper and colder. My legs started to ache. Wasn't this July? *Maybe we should get out*, I thought. But the rhododendrons on this section of riverbank were thick, leaning out over the water and allowing no exit. With Carsten on my back it would have been difficult to hack my way through. *No, better to stay on the river.*

I had lost all sense of time. We walked upriver in perpetual twilight, and I wanted it never to end. But soon we came upon a narrows leading into what appeared to be deep water. The rhododendron thickets overhung so far that we were forced into the river's middle. I moved out into the main current.

The water rose from calf-high to thigh-high to waist-high. Would we have to turn around?

I undid the straps on the backpack and swung Carsten around to my chest where I could see him. Little wispy shocks of blond fluttered on his head. He looked back at me with eyes the color of the pool, serene and trusting. We started walking into the pool. As I waded in I had to lift my son higher and higher, backpack and all: waist deep, stomach deep, chest deep until, in the middle of the pool, I held him above my head. It must have been strange for him to look down at

his father's body slowly sinking into the river until nothing re-
mained but two arms holding him aloft above an upturned,
worried face.

Surely Elizabeth was back at the cabin now, upriver beyond
shouting distance. Were I to stumble in that deep pool, should
the current prove too swift—perhaps it was risky to bring my
son here.

Upriver I could see a sandbar. If we can reach that, I
thought, we'll be safe.

This river had claimed one of Elizabeth's uncles. Bobo and
his brothers used to jump off a cliff next to First Falls where
the entire Tuckasegee drops thirty feet onto a pool below. On
one of those jumps Bobo drowned. He was eighteen.

The deepness of the pool before us, the seriousness of our
position—these kept me focused. I knew only that I was
chest-deep in water, holding Carsten above my head, and that
I couldn't slip.

Those thoughts coalesced into one driving desire: get to
the sandbar.

And we did. Soon we were standing in calf-deep water. I
slung my son around onto my back again, squeezed the tick-
lish spot on his knees. He giggled.

How foolish of me to bring him here.

When we exited the narrows we left the overhanging
rhododendrons choking out the last of the evening light and
came onto a wide stretch of river open to the sky. I stopped
for a moment, a long, delicious shiver tickling my spine. We
were safe. But at what risk? The full gravitas of our passage was
slapping me. It was the guilty knowledge that I had taken
chances with my son's—*our* son's—safety.

Yet for some reason I had been spared, catastrophe averted.
Like Dostoevsky in St. Petersburg before the Czar's firing

squad, I had been granted reprieve. Every step taken, every breath breathed in my son's presence from here on would be precious. Even though that pool wasn't life-threatening—I could have saved him had we gone under, I believe—the experience reminded me that every moment of my son's life was a gift.

Nothing but gift.

This was my blessing.

That it was undeserved was what in fact made it a blessing.

Our watery road opened before us like a spacious hallway of blue slate, as if built just for us. Cabin lights appeared up ahead. I knew this part of the river. There was the rope swing. Up a bit further was the plunge-pool where that very morning we had dunked before breakfast. That was the Clarke family rule. Be it December or July—if you wanted breakfast, you had to dunk for it.

We had come a long way, my son and I. Though I felt a great weariness, my legs numb from the cold and from carrying him upriver, it was a good kind of weary. The current had offered resistance, enough to make me feel like I was working to get somewhere. Working to find the blessing.

Fred Bahnson's poems and essays have appeared in Orion, The Sun, Fugue, Pilgrimage, *and the anthologies* Dance the Guns to Silence: 100 Poems for Ken Saro-Wiwa *and* Best American Spiritual Writing 2007. *He is the recipient of the 2006 Pilgrimage Essay Award and was the 2008 William Raney scholar in nonfiction at Bread Loaf Writer's Conference. He is currently a Food & Society policy fellow at the Institute for Agriculture and Trade Policy and a Senior Fellow at the Oakland Institute. He lives on a farm in the North Carolina mountains with his wife and two sons.*

MARK JENKINS

⋆ * ⋆

The Snowcave

*Snug in their winter den, a family kindles
the memory of a friend and father.*

THIS IS THE WAY WE IMAGINED IT, MIKE AND I. OUR KIDS
in the mountains together, just as we were when we were kids.
We talked about it whenever we were too far from home, on
expeditions, lying on our backs in the tent when we should
have been letting our bodies sleep.

Justin refuses to wear his backpack on his shoulders. It's
heavy because he brought his dinosaur books. He lets the
straps slip down to his elbows, binding his arms, so when he
trips he falls face first. He doesn't mind. It gives him a chance
to examine the bugs on the snow. Addi has her teddy bear and
two other stuffed animals who have names I don't know in
her pack, but wouldn't consider endangering them with a fall.
Addi and Justin are both in snowsuits, knit caps that keep slipping off, mittens already soaked. They're skiing, slowly, across
Lake Marie. They are both six years old, born a month apart.
They are the same height. They have the same red faces, the
same easy laugh, the same unquenchable curiosity. Justin collects insects, Addi collects rocks.

It is June in Wyoming at ten thousand feet. The snow is eight feet deep, the lakes still frozen. We are skiing together to the snowcave. We're going winter camping, an endeavor best done in summer—double the sunlight, triple the temperature. The snowcave is carved from the same drift Mike and I built caves in when we were boys. Of course it's not the identical drift but a descendant. A deep, beautiful drift in a long line of deep, beautiful drifts. Hidden in the lee of a glacial erratic the size of an apartment building, it took us years to find it.

When we get to the snowcave Justin and Addi can't get their skis off fast enough. They drop their packs and creep inside as if it were a tunnel into another world. The ceiling is over four feet high, which means they can stand up. They run their fingers along the chiseled walls and scuff the ice floor with their boots. Addi lies down, checking out the levelness of the sleeping platform. Justin discovers the air hole and sticks his arm up inside it. In the next two days the snowcave will be a secret hideout, a fortress, a bear's den, a spaceship.

We were older when Mike and I built our first snowcave but the enchantment was the same. It was a fort to us too, a hand-hewn refuge in the wilderness. Over the course of two decades we built all kinds of snowcaves. Miserable holes no self-respecting marmot would inhabit, circular lairs with sensual candlelight that inspired carnal speculations, burrows so far below the surface that snowmobiles roared over our roof without us knowing. One year, with the help of our younger brothers, we mined a cavern so expansive we played croquet. Upside down ice axes for mallets, bound wool socks for balls. Five days later the ceiling had sagged so far we had to use the ice axes as stanchions to hold it up.

When we were young and literal we believed winter camping was properly done in winter. Once, in high school, we set out in the dead of January in the coldest storm in a generation. Mike and I thought this good sport. In town it got down to 54 degrees below zero. We were thousands of feet higher and the wind was furious. Maybe it got down to absolute zero. Who knows? We were having too good a time to notice, snug as bugs in a rug in our snowcave. We brought enough food for an expedition and decided to stay a few extra days. By the time we got back home our families—traditionally stoic and optimistic about our misadventures—were frightened and mounting a rescue.

Not to romanticize snowcaves. They're too hard to build correctly and take too much time and energy. Nine out of ten times a tent is better. But that's not the point. Never was. We had tents even back then but what fun would that have been? A snowcave was the opportunity to build something. A chance to dig and crawl on your belly and get cold and wet. A chance to battle the elements, wield mortal weapons, prove how we could beat the odds no matter what they were. What more could Wyoming boys want?

At dusk, clouds fat as pregnant salmon swim through a darkling sky and Justin begins to howl. He cranes his head back and lets her rip. Addi joins in and they howl and then break into ordinary screaming. Trying to one up each other, they scream until their youthful throats grow rough. I don't stop them. If you can't scream your head off in the mountains, where can you? It's something I learned from Mike. He didn't worship mountains. Only people who've never spent much time in the mountains worship them. Like guys who never go on a date worship women. Live or work in the high country and you have to be more practical than that, other-wise you get killed.

When the moon slips out Addi and Justin insist on a ghost story. We are at the base of a black, thousand-foot wall of quartzite. It's called the Diamond. Mike and I used to attempt to climb it every winter, never succeeding. The cornices on the ridge have been breaking off all day—rumbling down the couloirs leaving piles of debris that look small and benign until you ski up to them and discover the blocks are bigger than trucks. I tell them that actually avalanches are started by ghosts. You can't see them, but they're up there, jumping up and down on the cornices, laughing.

"How did they get up there?" asks Justin.

"They climbed," I say.

"Ghosts are climbers," states Addi, as if it were obvious.

"And skiers," says Justin.

After kicking off a few avalanches the ghosts get the idea that it would be fun to slide down on one, so they do. They ride the avalanches like cowboys ride bulls. One arm waving in the air.

The ghosts slide right down the mountain into the lake, which is half-thawed.

"Right into the water!" shouts Justin, delighted.

"They like the cold because they don't get cold," explains Addi. "They're ghosts."

The story goes along, growing more and more complex, with lots of ad hoc events. It starts to get late.

At this point the ghosts discover two young snowcavers at the base of the mountain and naturally manage to lure them out into the dark. (Addi and Justin peer up at the dark massif overhead.) The ghosts want the two junior adventurers to come with them, into the everlasting unknown, but they are scared. They don't want to go. The ghosts start to pull on the children.

"I'm tired," says Addi.

"Me too," adds Justin quickly.

They unanimously decide to scurry into the snowcave and scooch down into their sleeping bags.

Before crawling in for the night I force both of them to relieve themselves, but it doesn't help. Too many cups of tomato soup and hot chocolate. Justin awakes at 2 A.M. To keep him from soiling or soaking his long johns, I make him strip off his underwear and crawl bare-assed out of the snowcave. He stands in the snow, alone in the moonlight with the clouds flying by like ghosts. Shooting back inside he dives into his sleeping bag and is instantly returned to sleep. Addi wakes at 3 A.M. and I make her do the same thing. Beyond the cave entrance I can see her squatting, staring warily up at the night sky.

In the morning I have a plan. I want us to climb Medicine Bow peak. I want them to want to climb Medicine Bow peak. They aren't interested. They want to go sledding. I remove the duffel bags and nylon straps from the haul sleds and they revert to what they were originally: five-dollar K-Mart kid sleds. Justin and Addi make only a few runs before wandering off to a newly-exposed creek. The creek winds back and forth around drifts before flowing into Lake Marie. The lake is entirely frozen except for a thin strip along the northern shore where this creek enters it. A scatter of angular rocks protrude from the glacial waters. It looks like a scene from the South Pole. We christen our discovery "Little Antarctica."

Addi and Justin begin hopping stone to stone above the icy water, first tentatively, then with growing boldness. At first they pretend they are penguins. Then decide they don't like penguins.

"Penguins are birds that can't fly," says Justin. He says he would rather be an Alaskan wolf and Addi thinks she would rather be an Eskimo girl fishing through holes in the ice. They both instinctively throw rock after rock into the slice of open water, fascinated by the blue-black liquid. Water is magic to children, the only substance they encounter in life that can be played with endlessly and never broken. Water will always go back to being what it was before they dropped it or stepped on it.

The water, although frigid, is only several feet deep. I admonish them not to fall in, then tramp back up to the snowcave to do chores. That's right. I leave two six-year-olds on the edge of a freezing lake in the middle of the mountains, alone.

Still, I pop my head out of the snowcave to check on them more often than I should. They are a ways off. I observe that Addi has a bit more balance than Justin—but more telling, is fearful of getting wet. She bounds above the water with concentration and precision. Justin on the other hand revels in being off-balance. After watching him slip off the rocks several times, his legs sinking up to his thighs in the ice-cold water before he drags himself out, I realize he's not slipping at all. He's doing it intentionally, just to see what will happen. From this distance I can't make out his mischievous grin, but I recognize it.

"Your muscles will freeze before you make it," I say.
"Bet they won't," counters Mike.
"Freeze solid and you'll sink like a rock."
Mike scoffs.
"Wanna bet?"
"Burrito dinner."

We shake on it. Mike strips in ten seconds and wades into Lake Marie bellowing homemade obscenities. When the water is up to his balls he dives in and begins swimming ferociously. The iceberg is floating in the middle of the lake, perhaps two hundred yards from shore. The snow around the lake is still three feet deep. July in the mountains of Wyoming. He plows out to the iceberg like a seal in the Arctic ocean. Next thing I know he has hauled himself up onto the iceberg and is dancing around on top, barefoot and buck-naked. Then he dives off and swims briskly back to shore. When he comes out of the gelid water, stomping footprints in the snow, his body is a bluish pink. He tries to give me his I-told-you-so smirk but the muscles in his face won't budge.

It is just after dawn. We are on our way to scale the Diamond. It takes Mike two full hours and five hundred feet of climbing to warm up.

Mike was the only man I knew who was an honest-to-God empiricist. He insisted on trying everything himself, as if it were impossible to learn anything except through first-hand experience. We were both like this; it was the genesis of our friendship. We inspired each other. Acts of profound stupidity were commonplace. Knowledge was to be gained by trial-and-error—not by listening to somebody tell us how or why or when we should or could or shouldn't or couldn't. When it came to the outdoors, we rarely consulted books. We were hell bent on reinventing the wheel. We became self-taught outdoorsmen. We taught ourselves how to ski, how to climb, how to backpack, how to build snowcaves. And for that reason it took us a long time to get good. Without instructors you learn very slowly. You make a lot of mistakes. What you're really learning is not the craft you're practicing. What are you learning?

You only realize it years afterward. Independence. Resourcefulness. Equanimity.

Later in the day we follow coyote tracks across the flank of the mountain. They are at least twelve hours old but Addi and Justin don't know that. The wily coyote could be behind the next boulder. They both want to know why all the trees are so short and look like flags, branches growing only on one side. I teach them the word *krummholtz* and try to explain the savagery of the wind, recounting another Mike-and-Mark adventure when both of us were right here, wearing huge winter climbing packs, and were lifted straight up off the ground.

Throughout the day I make them carry their own backpacks with their own water bottles and snacks. I make them rub the snot off their faces with the back of their mittens. I show them how to wipe with snow instead of toilet paper which leads to a hair-and-all discussion of alpine scatology.

In the afternoon we build a snowman and have a snowball fight. By then their snowsuits are soaked through and they're beginning to shiver. The wind has begun and bruised clouds are rolling overhead.

As I reload the sleds it begins to snow. We start the slow ski out to the car. Addi is the leader. She insists that her hands are not cold and that she doesn't have to put her gloves back on. Fine. Justin insists that his head is not cold and that he doesn't have to wear his wool cap. Fine.

We contour around the open water and head out over the frozen lake. As we shuffle along I try to get Justin to pull his pack up onto his shoulders but he insists on letting it fall down to his elbows and bang him on the back of the legs. For a moment I almost get angry. Then, suddenly, I laugh out loud. I throw my head back and look up into the moving sky and laugh. Justin skis up beside me.

"Watcha doing?"

I look over my shoulder at our ski tracks cutting onto the lake. I look ahead at Addi heading into the trackless snow. Justin is only six. I could make something up, but I don't.

"This is where we spread your Dad's ashes. Do you remember?"

Justin is excited. "We're skiing on my Dad ashes?"

I nod.

Somehow this seems wonderful to Justin, as if he were once again riding on Mike's shoulders.

Mike Moe, Dan Moe, Sharon Kava, and Brad Humphrey died on an expedition to the Arctic on September 1, 1995. Mark Jenkins also contributed "From the Mouths of Babes" to this collection.

JIM SPENCER

* * *

Bobble Your Stopper and Wiggle Your Piminnow

No, Daddy, you do it like this...

"I GOT ONE, DADDY! I GOT ONE!"

That excited pair of sentences burst from the lips of my tangle-haired nine-year-old daughter one long ago spring afternoon. We were fishing a small oxbow lake in the lower White River bottoms in southeast Arkansas. What got Alicia all worked up was the unexpected spectacle of a very respectable crappie flopping wildly on the otherwise calm lake surface near our small boat.

The crappie was firmly (I hoped) attached to the gold hook at the end of her line. Evidently that was indeed the case, because Alicia landed it per her usual technique—hauling back on her limber pole until the fish was airborne, then derricking it over the boat by brute force, yelling her head off all the while. After three abortive tries, I managed to grab her line as the frantically flopping critter sailed by my face yet again.

"It's a big one, Daddy!" Alicia screeched from her position approximately two feet off my right ear. "It's a lot bigger than yours." It's an exaggeration—but not much of one—when I say you could have heard her in downtown St. Charles, seven miles away across the vast bottomland forest.

She was right, though, on both counts: It *was* a big one, a heck of a lot bigger than the eight-incher I'd caught ten minutes earlier.

While I strung the piscatorial giant and rebaited my daughter's hook with another lively shiner, she regaled her brother Geoff and me with a spirited, detailed account of how she had managed to single-handedly overpower this burly, outsized fish that now tugged futilely at the frayed piece of nylon ski rope we were using for a stringer. (I had forgotten to bring a store-bought stringer; I almost always forget, although over the course of my fishing career I have probably purchased a mile of them.)

When I finished restoring her rig to fish-catching condition, Alicia picked up the pole and complacently flapped her hook back into the water. Then she started giving Geoff and me a detailed course of instructions on how to go about trying to duplicate her feat:

"Look. You don't have to fish up close to trees and stuff to catch a big fish. I caught mine right out here in the middle.

"Hold your pole up high like this, Daddy. You're holding yours too low, and it takes you too much time to raise it up when you get a bite.

"Move your stopper up higher on your string, Geoff. The fish can see it if you don't, and they get scared and swim off somewhere else.

"If your piminnow doesn't want to wiggle, then bobble your stopper up and down like this, to make it look like he is. (Alicia used to call minnows "piminnows." As a matter of fact, at twenty-eight, she still does.)

"You have to be a real good fisher to catch a big fish like that one I caught. I'll bet there aren't any more big ones like that left in this lake."

She was wrong about that one, though, because shortly after she spoke those words, her "stopper" bobbled and disappeared, and more screeching commenced. In a very few seconds, I was making grabs at another crappie that was the twin of her first one. And if Geoff and I thought Alicia had been lording it over us before, then we, too, were wrong.

"I don't believe I ever saw even a picture of two fish as big as those two are," she smugly informed us as I strung her second crappie on top of the first. "I don't think anybody ever, ever caught two fish that big on the same fishing trip."

And then we got another earful from Super-Fisherwoman: "Daddy, if you'll just move your pole back and forth a little, like this, you might catch one. But it won't be as big as my two are.

"No, no, Geoff. Your stopper is still too far down on your string. You're not ever going to catch a fish that way.

"If you two would stop losing so many piminnows, maybe I could catch a big fish for each of you. But not if you use all the piminnows up.

"Daddy, you're still not paying attention to what I'm telling you. You're still holding your pole too low. Hold it up high, like this. *And move it back and forth a little.* "

She sat there placidly, my bright and lovely daughter, casting these pearls of wisdom before us two swine with all the calm confidence of Billy Graham addressing a football stadium full of sinners. By the time the sun sank below the treeline and it was—mercifully—time to go, Geoff and I had even managed to catch a fish or two ourselves. Geoff caught a channel catfish considerably bigger than either of Alicia's two slab crappie. However, Alicia was quick to ask how big a crappie could get, and how big a catfish could get, and so on, until she had determined her one-and-a-half pound crappie were actually much bigger, comparatively speaking, than Geoff's three-pound catfish.

I caught nothing but runts, so all I rated was a better-luck-next-time pep talk from Alicia as I wound the line around her pole at the boat landing. It reminded me of several dugout speeches I've heard various baseball coaches make during my youth, usually just after we'd blown a crucial game.

But who knows, I thought, *maybe I actually will have better luck next time.* After all, thanks to Alicia's coaching, I now knew what I'd been doing wrong.

I was holding my pole too low, for one thing, and I think my stopper might have been too far down on my string. My piminnow wasn't very lively, either, and I neglected to bobble my stopper up and down or move my pole back and forth. On top of all that, I fished too close to trees and stuff.

I think I've got it all sorted out now, I remember thinking as I drove home that night, while Alicia slept peacefully in the back seat. *Fishing is a lot more complicated than I thought.*

After a career as a wildlife biologist and communications specialist, Jim Spencer retired from the Arkansas Game and Fish Commission and moved to the Ozark Mountains of north Arkansas, where he continues to write books, newspaper columns, and magazine articles about hunting, fishing, trapping, natural history, and the outdoors in general.

JENNIFER BOVÉ

* * *

A Place Among Elk

*Tracking elk while eight months pregnant, a new mother-to-be
redefines her place in the wild.*

WE'RE ONLY WEARING LONG JOHNS AND PAC BOOTS WHEN
we arrive at the turnout on Fisher Hill Road, just outside of
Glenwood, Washington. Our motley assortment of fleece,
flannel, and camouflage is reserved in a bag with cedar bark so
as not to absorb the scent of anything remotely human.
Tonight is the night. I am sure of this because it is Sunday, and
Chris has an early meeting with the Natural Resource
Conservation Service tomorrow morning. I, however, will not
be getting up for work with him anymore. Two days ago, I
celebrated the first day of my eighth month of pregnancy and
the last day of my foreseeable career as a field biologist for the
U.S. Fish and Wildlife Service.

Chris parks the truck beneath the heavy boughs of the
Doug fir we've come to recognize like a friend and opens the
door to the cold. As he begins to unload our gear, I shuffle behind the truck. Ours is the only set of tire tracks in the new
dusting of snow, but a girl likes her privacy just in case.

"Announcing our arrival?" he whispers as I crouch awkwardly beside the tire.

I can't look at him or I will start giggling, so I stare at a scattering of raven tracks on the ground.

"At least I won't need to go in the woods."

Chris bundles up in underclothes and camouflage as fast as he can stuff his shivering limbs into them, and he secures his pants with an old skull and crossbones belt buckle. It's a tradition. He reaches out a hand to help me up, and he smiles.

"Missed your boots this time, I hope?"

I give him a shove. "Yeah, thanks. Now will you shut up? You're gonna scare my elk away."

He passes me my flannel pants, sweater, jacket, and the camouflage coveralls that are just barely big enough to accommodate me. This suit is the closest thing I've got to maternity camo, and I wriggle into it like a snake trying to get back into its skin. With my gloves tucked perfectly into my sleeves, I can't get a grip on the zipper, so Chris closes the coveralls over my bulging middle, stretching the material tight. We look at each other and grin. He leans down with his hands cupped on either side of my belly and whispers something I can't quite hear.

Each of us dons a wool hat, and Chris stuffs the ends of my scarf into my collar. I take a pinch of baking soda to swish around in my mouth if for no other reason than it makes us *believe* we are scentless. He grabs his compound, and I sling my recurve and quiver over my shoulder. We double-check our pockets for flashlights, lighters, compass, trail flagging, and the cell phone.

Daylight is fading.

We cross the road and find the broken wire in the fence. Our footprints from last weekend have been erased by snowfall, and now there are large cloven tracks on either side of the fence that suggest the herd's passage earlier today. I point to a tuft of sand-colored hair wedged into a barb, and Chris nods. If instinct serves us, they are not far.

Chris drops and slides beneath the bottom wire. As he holds it up a few more inches for me, I do a clumsy knees-and-elbows scoot underneath, careful not to snag my bow on the barbs. He helps me stand and brushes snow from my coveralls.

"You're beautiful," he whispers.

I give him a quick kiss, and crystalline droplets of breath that have already begun to condense on his mustache wet my upper lip.

We march onward, deeper into a grove of stark and skeletal scrub oaks. Our steps are as light and swift as is possible in pac boots, and the new snow is mercifully soft. When we reach the edge of the old-growth conifer stand, we survey the snow for tracks. Scant turkey and a lone blacktail. Just a few paces inside the treeline, though, we discover a generous pile of marble-sized droppings. Definitely elk. Chris picks up a piece and it crumbles between his fingers. Definitely not fresh. We rub our boot soles in the pile anyway, and then we move on.

Within the big woods, we wind along our own familiar path because evidence of the herd's presence is sketchy and tough to follow. The dense forest canopy has filtered the morning's snow into a mosaic of white islands that cautious animals seem to carefully avoid. Fresh track upon fallen sticks and frozen ground are difficult even for a couple of biologists to discern.

Fortunately, the terrain rolls gently from ridge to draw, as I'm not up for much hill-humping anymore. I wrap my hand under my belly for support and comfort. It is weighing heavy tonight, aching near my pelvis like it does frequently these days, and as I walk, I send soothing thoughts to the mysterious little one within.

Rest easy, I tell her, *it's not time for you to stir just yet.*

Finally, after a good mile or two, I spy the clearing ahead. At its far eastern rim, a bright semicircle of sunshine still rings the open meadow and washes the surrounding trees in gold. We are just in time. Chris taps my shoulder, and I stop to look at him. He points to his ear. I am breathing hard, so I take a gulp of air and hold it so I can listen.

The distant snap of a twig splinters the icy quiet.

Chris's blue eyes are locked on mine, and we stand as still as the air.

There is a brushing sound from the trees and then the beating of broad wings—no doubt a turkey roused from its roost.

I continue to lead the way to our secret niche. Now that it is so close to my due date, Chris refuses to let me out of his sight, so we had to find a place where we could hide together. Of course I protested, insisting we'd never see an animal— much less get a shot at one—unless we separated. He wouldn't hear of it, though, and he can be as stubborn as stone.

Chris takes his place among a tight trio of cedars, and I lower myself onto a mound of exposed dirt beside an up-turned root wad that serves as a crude blind. On the other side of the downed tree is an elk trail that, although recently used, bears no blemish of prints tonight. It is simply a curving ribbon of dusted snow along which we anticipate the elk will travel.

I pull the glove off my right hand with my teeth so that I can wet my index finger with saliva, and I see Chris doing the same thing. We hold our fingers up in synchrony to the air for some indication of motion. My finger feels almost uniformly chilled, but if there is even the slightest breeze, it is from the east and shouldn't betray us.

I watch Chris for a moment. How many times have I observed him like this in the woods? He scuffs the ground with his boots to move leaves and debris aside. He places another pinch of baking soda on his tongue. He readies his release and pulls his facemask down. Then, he gives me a wink and nestles against the ragged cedar trunks, broad shoulders becoming burls and bow blending into brush.

I move a rock out from under me and settle as comfortably as I can beside the underbelly of the fallen tree. I am still warm from the hike, but I keep my left glove on and slide my scarf up over my face because it will get nothing but colder while I pose motionless, as if asleep. My leather finger tab is stiff in my bare hand so I clench my fist a couple of times to break it in and check my draw length to make sure I have room to pull back my string. Chris pats my head, and I give him a wink back.

I think I'm ready.

The woods are hushed. They, too, seem to hold their breath and listen, waiting for movement. But we do not move. I feel tendrils of patience unfurling as I relax, twining to bark and soil. I study my surroundings—linear edges of tree trunks, the subtle dappling of light on a rust brown rock, and the arch of a bulbous root against a jagged pattern of frost-tinged grass. It is these lovely minutiae I think I miss most as an adult. When I was closer to the ground, I knew the secrets of nature's detail.

Gripping my bow, an arrow knocked, it is still a little surprising to find myself in the role of hunter. I was a self-proclaimed animal activist and devout vegetarian throughout college, and I thought that researching wildlife thereafter made me some sort of an expert on wilderness and hunters and cruelty. It was not until I accompanied Chris on our first

whitetail hunt that I understood the extent to which my love
for nature had been that of an outsider. I began shadowing
Chris more often, as a curious observer and student of his
skill, and I came to immerse myself in the ways of the animals.
As I witnessed the beauty of the ritual, I stepped down from
a soapbox built by people who long ago buried their roots beneath concrete, and I began to understand that true hunting
has far more to do with patience and awe than bloodlust, and
that death in the absence of fear or suffering is not cruel. So I
guess it was only a matter of time before I assumed a bow and
my own identity on our expeditions. I wanted to join the circle. Now, in my debut season as a huntress, I also carry our first
baby, and her presence fills me with purpose. I am an animal
mother, wild with child.

As the forest releases its breath, I begin to hear twittering
juncos and the *pik* of a downy woodpecker. It seems Chris and
I are no longer cause for suspicion—the predators have vanished. I raise my gaze from the ground to see that the halo of
sun has faded from the clearing, and with it has fled the fickle
warmth of the afternoon. Shapes and lines have smudged into
nuances of shadow, transforming my field of vision into a confusing chiaroscuro until my eyes adjust. The air smells like
frozen evergreen and sleeping earth through the thick weave
of my scarf. It won't be long now.

Dusk will spur the herd. I picture them rising from their
beds and mulling around the darkening woods, chirping in
low tones of familiarity. One member, an aging cow perhaps,
will grow restless. Experience has taught her the signs of safety,
and I pray she will sense no danger tonight. The matriarch
will strike out along a well-trodden path, leading the others
toward this open feeding ground. The herd bull will lumber
behind them, slower and more apprehensive now that the rut
has ended. I remember his chocolate mane and widely

branched antlers perfectly from my glimpse of him in September, and the fevered clarity of his bugle still rings in my ears. I am sure, if he eluded the onslaught of rifle season, that the bull is now more keenly attuned to the threat of hunters. With any luck he, too, will remain at ease, and the dark caravan will draw close to where we hide.

Time passes slowly as we wait, the minutes more viscous in the deepening cold. I am all too aware that the slightest influence may cause the herd's routine to shift, that they may not come at all. Countless hours in the woods have taught me that while humans operate on graceless schedules, elk dance to the rhythm of intuition.

An audible sigh escapes my lips, muffling the sound of a branch breaking somewhere west of us—I can't begin to guess how far. Another moment oozes by, long enough for my conscience to start cussing at me for being careless and potentially blowing our cover, and then I hear it again. It must be the footfall of an animal.

I steal a peek at Chris from the corner of my eye. His gaze is intent on the direction of the sound and his elbow is cocked, ready to draw. I constrict my grip around the bow's riser.

Am I ready?

My heart flutters like a trapped moth even though I know the sound does not necessarily indicate elk. It could be anything from a hefty porcupine to a black bear with a case of early winter insomnia. Images flash through my mind of a 350-pound bear ambling toward us, his pliant nose tugging scents from the air. Would he smell us beneath the baking soda? And if he did, would he approach? An unfamiliar sensation of vulnerability surges hot to my chest. I have never been scared of bears, but pregnancy has changed my perspective on a lot of things. I am acutely conscious of how difficult it would be to shield my belly in the rare event of an attack, and running isn't even a consideration.

I wonder how quickly an arrow would stop a bear.

But whatever kind of creature I might have heard seems to slip away without even a rustle to indicate its retreat, and I am left to wait again in the lingering gray of dusk. I'm getting colder by the minute; the chill of the ground is seeping through my boots and multiple socks to my toes and up into my calves. I wrinkle my nose and the creases are reluctant to smooth. My stomach is growling, quietly for the time being, and on top of the rest I am fighting the urge to yawn. However tightly I cling to my newfound hunter's resolve, I recognize these symptoms as the onset of doubt.

I lean forward slowly, one centimeter at a time, to regain some semblance of a vigilant posture and to rest my belly between my legs. In this position, one of my thighs ends up high-centered on a knobby root or rock that will inevitably begin to deaden my sciatic nerve if I don't shift my legs, but I bite the inside of my cheek and resist the urge to move it. There can be no allowance for the indiscretions of my impatience now that elk season is nearing its end and we have no meat.

Focus, I tell myself, *focus*.

"So, are you ready to go?" Chris whispers.

I turn to him, aghast. "What?"

"I'm hungry, aren't you? Anyway, I don't feel like it's gonna happen tonight." He takes a step away from the tree where he'd been leaning.

He knows how easy I am to sway (as pathetic as that may be) when it's freezing and the prospect of food is involved, so even though we'll both feel guilty about it later, I just shrug and lurch to my knees. So much for focus and resolve. Pausing with my bow planted in preparation to pull myself up, my eyes are enticed around the fallen tree by the outline of a tear-shaped silhouette. Chris is replacing his arrow in its quiver, which he rarely does before we're out of the woods, as I trace the dark shape downward into the curve of a long neck and realize I'm staring at an elk cow not even a hundred yards away.

"O.K.," I whisper. "But I have a different feeling."

Incredibly, the cow seems completely unaware of our commotion because she is heading right for us at an easy gait, and there are others following her. I don't know how I didn't hear them before, tromping along like a bunch of cattle. Despite their amazing agility, they are heavy on the hoof and crush deadfall noisily as they move through the woods.

Chris stiffens, knowing he can't risk pulling out an arrow—the cow is too close. I just keep kneeling there, clutching my bow with such intensity that I begin to tremble. My scarf has slipped from my face, which is surely glaring like a beacon through the veil of dusk, and I am jutting from the forest floor in plain sight, an incongruous figure in a realm the elk know intimately. I need to raise the bow several inches in order to draw, and there is no real reason I should not try it. I tell myself to pull back the string, sight in on the cow's lungs, and let the arrow fly with the same confidence I possess when I shoot targets. I am a good shot, consistent and accurate. But the cow is now less than thirty clear yards from me with a calf, a second cow, and possibly more of the herd behind her. There is no question one of them would see me move. If the cow were to stop or sidestep or bolt, I could wound her.

And so I can't. I can't do it.

Blood is throbbing in my ears so loudly that I fear the elk will feel the resonant beat like thunder through the ground. The cow, glorious in her tawny winter coat and every bit as big as a mare, traipses past me on the narrow trail. She is within twenty feet, so close I see the auburn tips of her mane and a healed scar across her foreleg, so close I can smell her heady musk. I am certain she will notice me and startle at any second, but she is fixed on the clearing ahead. She doesn't bat an eye.

The second cow strays from the trail and moves alongside of the first, and I think I might be able to get a shot at her from this angle, but something tickles the calf's curiosity and he steps toward me with his head lowered, attentive to secrets the ground might tell. Each careful placement of his chiseled hooves brings him boldly closer to the strange new tree stump that must bear the smell, if ever so faint, of a different animal. The calf's wide amber eyes roll from side to side, and I could nearly reach out and touch the wetness gleaming in the bowl of his flared nostril. I keep painstakingly steady, though, breathing no more deeply than leaves. I have to remind myself that I am not, nor have I ever been, one of his herd. However burdened I might be by the persistence of empathy, however desperately I might long to run with him, just once, I am the predator.

The youngster turns casually, clambers over a tree limb, and then stops to sniff it. Any seasoned hunter would take advantage of this situation somehow, and I know Chris is so crazy watching all of this that he's considering taking my arrow and plunging it into any one of these elk by hand, but I am new at the game—I am still soft.

One of the cows, who has paused at the edge of the clearing, mews sharply. The calf raises his head and begins to plod away reluctantly, barely missing the toe of Chris's boot. That's when I glimpse the other cow standing fifteen or twenty yards beyond the three cedars. She is mostly hidden behind the trees so that all I can see are pieces of her—the hump of her shoulder and a stout hind flank fringed in creamy light fur. This time, maybe because my chances are better or more than likely because I know she is the one without a calf, I dare to twist my body and thrust the bow out in front of me, brushing Chris's pant leg. My best bet is to aim through the trees so that when she moves I am guaranteed a lung shot. With my left eye squeezed shut, I stretch the string back to the corner of my mouth, steady my broadhead in the open V between the cedars, and I hold.

One of the other elk snorts, and I hear the uneasy shuffle of hooves. They must have seen me draw. My shoulder is burning, and the muscles in my belly are strained. The cow moves forward just enough for me to sight in on the broad barrel of her ribcage, and in that chaotic instant before I decide to release my arrow, I hear the other two bolt. The cow wheels and lunges furiously into the woods, and even if I could have wrenched my torso another inch, I never would have been able to take a shot.

It's over.

I let the bow fall from my frigid fingers and slide the arrow into my quiver. Chris remains silent as I grab his jacket to pull myself up.

All I can think to say is: "I missed my chance before."

He still doesn't speak, and maybe for the first time ever, I'm not sure exactly what he's thinking. Then he hugs me and starts to laugh.

"What's so damn funny?"

"Nothin'," he chuckles. "I'm just proud of you, my tough, crazy, pregnant wife."

My face breaks into an uncontainable grin. "I was good, then, huh? I was invisible."

"Yeah, you were." He looks at me and frowns. "But I don't understand why you wanted to give up so early..."

"Oh, no—you're not pinning that one on me," I try to tell him seriously, but I can't keep a straight face. We may be leaving empty-handed, but my spirits are high.

Reaching down to pick up my bow, I feel the baby awaken and start to squirm, so I rub the curve of her back where it protrudes from my stomach and shiver just a little. On some level deep beneath civility or compassion, I am exhilarated by my pursuit of wild and wary prey. I found a place within the circle tonight. Here among the elk, I realize, guilt is of no consequence and there is no such thing as sin.

"You O.K.?" Chris asks.

"Yes," I assure him, "I am."

"Well, then what do you say we go get something to eat?" He takes my bow and quiver and tosses them onto his shoulder.

"I say it's about time. I'm starving."

Hand-in-hand, we hike back to the road by the light of a luminous moon, feeling our way gingerly along the path. When we get to the truck, we will peel off our layers, crank the heater, and ease into the pleasure of thawing. Chris will slide a Townes Van Zandt cassette into the tape deck, and once we are revived on the warm ride to town, we will begin to reflect on the hunt. Descriptions will flow fast and full like a river in flood, coursing through bottomless bowls of chowder beside the woodstove at the Shade Tree Inn. Our shared images will grow over time into a living, breathing entity with bones of truth and the blood of reminiscence. Such, I imagine, is the birth of any good story, any good life.

Jennifer Bové also contributed "Den Mother" to this collection.

* * *

The Facts of Life

*Life's most valuable lessons don't always
make for polite conversation.*

SCHOOL BEGAN JUST AS THE MONSOON SEASON CAME TO
an end, so when the rains stopped it was time to head back
home. My husband was working on his dissertation, studying
amphibians in the Chihuahuan Desert. We packed up another
summer's worth of field gear and drove from the southwest-
ern tip of Texas, right across the river from Mexico, to the
eastern side of the state. From dry stick and bone to moist
green and mildew—all in one state. The heat never faltered.

Our daughter Savanna was starting preschool that year. On
the first day I stood around the playground with the other
parents, watching with fear and pride as our toddlers morphed
into kids—playing tag, throwing balls, dangling from monkey
bars. Just as I commented on how grown-up our children
looked, my daughter pulled down her pants and peed in the
sand box.

"I'm sorry," I said sheepishly, "She was potty trained while
we were in the field doing research, so she learned to go outside before she learned to use a toilet." The other moms
looked at me like I had just said we didn't have indoor

plumbing and I thought, *Come on ladies, this is preschool.* I didn't tell them she actually *preferred* to pee outside; when she had to go, she would race through the front door and squat on the lawn. When I tried to explain that if a toilet was available we usually went *inside*, she would insist, "No! I go pee-pee outside. Like doggies."

Secretly I was proud. My daughter wasn't afraid to pee outside—like she wasn't afraid of tarantulas or rat snakes or giant rhinoceros beetles. She loved to dress up like a princess in ruffles and tulle, and was attracted to all things pink and sparkly, but she could stomp through mud to catch a toad and didn't squirm when a garter snake musked her. A girl who might one day wear hiking boots beneath her prom gown.

Because her father and I met in the field—both biologists at the time, studying frogs and salamanders in the Pacific Northwest—it seemed inevitable that our children would be comfortable sleeping outdoors, scrambling up scree slopes, and pulling critters from muddy creeks. Savanna was conceived while my husband was just beginning to collect data in Big Bend National Park. So much of my pregnancy was spent chasing storm clouds across the vast Chihuahuan Desert, bouncing around in four-wheel drive without A/C, and praying that I wouldn't go into premature labor because we were two hours from the nearest hospital.

We lived in researcher quarters during those summers, an adobe ranch house shaded by a rock outcrop and surrounded by nothing but vast desert. It had a great porch with a view of the Sierra del Carmen mountains. We kept a little pool filled with hose water and animals would come across the parched land to drink. Bobcats, coyote, deer, and whole herds of javelina came to wet their muzzles. When I was hugely pregnant, I would sit out there and gaze at the Carmens glowing rose and gold in the refracted rays of the setting sun, and I'd think of all the amazing things in this world that I couldn't wait to show to the unborn child who rolled in the ocean of my belly.

Savanna went on her first camping trip when she was four months old. We bundled her in fleece and placed her in a little cardboard box so we wouldn't smother her between our down bags in the tent. It was December, Christmas break, and the desert can get cold in the winter. I remember how I woke every hour throughout the night, holding my hand to her chest to make sure she was still breathing. In the morning I carried her in a sling as we hiked through boulders. Her wide eyes reflected the brazen sky. Cradled to my breast, she looked out at talus slopes and slender ocotillo, at ravens that arced through the blue, and I was happy that this scene was one of the earliest she would have imprinted in her brain.

We spent every summer, and many spring and winter breaks, in Big Bend. It was a ten-hour drive from our house, but somehow it felt as though the desert *was* our home. Our other house—the little fixer-upper painted bright yellow in the small town on the other side of the state—was simply a way station, a place we lived and worked between field seasons, instead of the other way around. So, naturally, Savanna learned to crawl in the desert. I winced as she dodged cholla spines and scorpions. First I feared rattlesnakes, and then, once she was faster, I feared mountain lions—she was about the size of a baby javelina. Inside, the researcher house wasn't much safer because there she had to maneuver through an obstacle course of formalin-filled vials, dissecting scalpels, and mouse droppings, not to mention the occasional scorpion that would scuttle through the gap beneath the door. She was never left alone. I stood by like a shadow she didn't know was there as she explored rocks, bugs, and delicate flowers growing in cracks of desert pavement.

In those early days, Savanna passed many hours in the baby backpack while her daddy and I hiked through the desert surveying for amphibians, collecting microhabitat data, and searching for springs, *tinajas,* and old cattle tanks that would hold water. She took most of her naps during long rides in the car seat as we jostled down washboard roads. She learned to stop and look when she heard the hissing rattle of a western diamondback and to carefully back away once she spotted it. When we saw a tarantula ambling along, she would let the huge hairy spider creep up her fingers, tickling the skin on her forearms. Our favorite picture of her is the one where she has a Transpecos rat snake draped across her head, its body curling down past her baby-toothed smile to outstretched hands.

The natural world was so *normal* to her—just a part of her life like a cup of milk with dinner and story time before bed. Her first words, after *Dada* and *Mama,* were *moon* and *gecko.* On her third birthday, as I lit the candles on her cake, a herd of javelina came snorting and snuffing into our yard. The adults were in the lead and babies in tow, waddling on awkward legs. When she saw them through the window, she grinned and said, "Oh, look! The javelina are coming to my birthday party!" If a thunderstorm was brewing, the sky dense with gray and the smell of ozone, Savanna would jump up and down and holler "Yahoo! Rain's coming! That means frogs and toads!"

And if it really was a good storm, we'd chase the thunderheads across the desert (lightning streaks, flash floods, smell of wet creosote) listening for the trill of narrow-mouthed toads calling, or the deep sheep-like bleating of spadefoot toads. We followed the sounds to the breeding pool where males called out to the females across the desert. Savanna was always right beside us in the mud that stuck to our legs like plaster, pulling toads from the murky pools, stomping in the water that swirled like a puddle of chocolate milk around her toddler thighs. She learned to say *Bufo debilis* instead of green toad, *Scaphiopus* instead of spadefoot.

We went out at night with headlamps and Savanna watched thoughtfully from behind the beam of her light as the males battled for females, shoving each other and wrestling cartoon-like in the mud. The males' vocal sacs would inflate exactly like balloons as they called out—the biggest and loudest call attracting the most females. When a victor finally grasped a female (sometimes after several false attempts at mating with other angry males), he would hold on tight with pudgy arms, riding the female's back as the pair swam around the pool in amplexus. The noise was deafening. You would hear it from miles away in the desert flats, and long after you left the breeding pool it would hum in your ears like a buzzing gnat that won't go away.

"Mommy, why are they riding piggyback?" Savanna asked the first time she saw this dance of life. I explained they were making babies—the female lays eggs as the male rides her back, squirting sperm on the eggs. When the sperm and the eggs combine, they make tadpoles. "Oh," she said, inquisitive eyes studying the toads in their struggle to carry on their genes in the pool (literally and figuratively).

During the days and weeks that followed, we returned to breeding pools and watched as the eggs developed and hatched into larvae. We watched as tiny tadpoles squirmed around, yolk sacs still attached, then as they absorbed their sacs and their tails and began to sprout tiny legs. As the ephemeral pools grew smaller beneath the scorching sun, we watched tiny copper-colored toadlets hop away to find refuge beneath rocks or burrow down in the mud. We also watched as other pools dried up and thousands of tadpoles died before they metamorphosed, squirming, struggling, eventually still.

Nothing left but bent twigs in the shape of tadpoles embedded in the cracked mud.

"Mommy, that's sad," Savanna said and I agreed, though I told her this was the way of life. I tossed the word "natural selection" into the air, knowing it would be years before she'd really understand.

When children grow up outdoors, spending a lot of time around nature and animals, they do not question the facts of life. Just as a child raised on a ranch knows what it means when a stallion goes out to stud and isn't squeamish about preg-checking the cows, a child raised by field biologists soon becomes aware that sexual reproduction is the driving force of life.

During that first year of preschool, after everyone had recovered from the sandbox incident, I was lingering in the play yard again, talking to some of the other moms. Our kids were chasing each other and laughing. One little boy jumped piggy-back on a little girl. Savanna shouted out, "Look Mama! Pretty soon he's gonna spray her eggs with sperm, and then they're going to have a baby!"

We didn't get a lot of play dates that year. But it didn't matter because when the field season rolled around again, we were back in the desert, chasing thunderstorms and listening for Texas toads calling us home.

Lily Dayton is a freelance writer who has worked as a field biologist in the Pacific Northwest, Southern California, North Carolina, West Texas, and Mexico. She received her bachelor's degree in Zoology from Humboldt State University and her master's degree in Education from Texas A&M University. She currently lives in Santa Cruz, California, where she spends as much time as possible outside with her two young daughters.

⋆ ⋆ ⋆

Migration

Up north, weather can be a wilderness all its own.

THE TERMINAL, A LONG GRAY HALL WITH PINBALL MACHINES at the far end, was almost empty when we arrived. We were late because of the weather report we had heard, but the plane wouldn't leave without us since we were its only passengers that morning. There were six of us: our family of five and Ron, our longtime fisherman friend, constituting a full flight for the Piper Cherokee we were chartering. I was pregnant with our fourth child, someone we didn't know yet but were anxious to meet.

The pilot watched as we stumbled into the hall with boxes and bulging black garbage bags for luggage. He looked at us questioningly. We knew him from years in a small Alaskan town, from countless flights before.

"You're going out to Larsen Bay this morning?" he asked, puzzled.

"Yeah, we're going to fish camp for the week," Duncan answered.

"The weather's good now, but have you heard the forecast?"

"We heard yesterday it's supposed to blow Southeast 60."

"How about Southeast 80 to 100?" the pilot said with a subtle lift of his eyebrows. For a bush pilot, it was the equivalent of wild gesticulations.

This was news. I raised my eyebrows too. But how much worse is 80- or 90-mile-an-hour wind than 60?

"Why are you going out there this time of year?" he asked, looking at the children.

"For spring break," I replied as blithely as possible, trying to sound like a happy vacationer. The careful listener would have heard a hint of sarcasm.

It had not been my idea. To spend spring break at fish camp on Harvester Island sounded to me like coal miners picnicking down in the shafts. One friend was going to Greece for spring break. Other years we had gone to Hawaii, to Florida, to Mexico. It wasn't the ideal pregnancy vacation, but the kids were excited and, knowing nothing of Hawaii, wanted to go to fish camp more than anywhere else. Gradually, I began to see the sense of it. This time we would go and just play, and maybe when we got tired of that, work on the many projects we never got to in the summer. High on my list was a plumbing system and running water. That idea alone sold me on the trip.

But now, 80 to 100? Kodiak sees blows like that at least once a year, but we don't usually plan a vacation around them. Still, the weather was clear and calm as we stood there. It was cold, about 8 degrees, but the winds were either still traveling, or had veered off elsewhere.

Duncan and I watched each other, figuring. The flight was only thirty-five minutes. We would be there within the hour. Once there, in the village, we had to launch our skiff, then make the final leg—a thirty-minute ride out to the island. If all went well, we could be on the island in three hours.

"What do you think?" Duncan broke the silence, addressing the pilot. "We can beat it if we leave this morning, don't you think? It won't hit until later today."

"Yeah, if we go right now we'll probably beat it," he agreed.

Duncan looked at me.

"Let's go!" I said, agreeing, confident we could get there first.

By the time we landed in Larsen Bay, the wind had begun, a biting, insistent breeze that promised more. An hour and a half later, the skiff had been launched and we were on our way. The breeze was now a genuine *blow*. At 8 degrees, with our course headlong into a 30-knot wind, I didn't need a wind chill chart to know it was bitter cold. We all wore almost our entire closet of winter clothing, still the wind sent us under a tarp, huddled together, backs walled against the gale. Isaac, our two-year-old, sat on my knees. Noah, six, pressed against my side with my arm cinched around him for comfort and warmth. Seven-year-old Naphtali sandwiched herself between Noah and Ron. Duncan ran the skiff, standing upright in the stern to see over the high bow.

The trip was longer than usual. Halfway through, feeling less embattled, I poked my head from the tarp and caught my breath. The wind was tearing the top of the waves off, the spume spilling out so white—so blindingly white—and the sun a vacation sun. There was no warmth in it, only icy brightness, but it lit the work of the wind, igniting colors. And later, as we rounded the last cape, we saw whales spouting; the tempest seemed for that moment only a unanimous frolic.

The wind steadily increased the rest of the day. We were on solid ground by then, safe on our island, but we were not warm. The house was 5 degrees inside. With every heat source flaming—the wood stove, all burners of the propane gas stove, the propane heater, the oil stove—it took twelve hours to warm just the front room to 50 degrees. We were proud of how tightly we had built the house, the insulation, the thick walls, the Anderson windows. But that day, and the next two, the walls felt like cheesecloth. The wind hissed through the window moldings and wailed through the doorjambs, devouring our heat as fast as we could make it.

We didn't sleep much that night, the kids piled up on one bed, the adults on couches in the one warm room. The stovepipe to the woodstove, rising twelve feet above us, cranked and shimmied with every blast of wind, threatening rupture and fire at every moment. The nearest person was eight miles away by water, not that it mattered. Had we been only half a mile from a neighbor, no one could've moved. All the world was paralyzed, pinned to the ground.

By morning, we guessed the wind to be near the 100 mark, the wind chill about 70 below. The vista out our front windows was unrecognizable. The distinctive colors of browns, whites, blues, and grays had blurred into a single color: the color of wind, a streaked white erasing all boundaries between elements of water, sky, clouds, mountains, air, house. All dissolved into howl and smoke, moan and scream.

For three days we read, sang Mother Goose with the kids, nursed and voodooed our heat sources, and hunched in front of the windows, watching. We saw our own insignificance, and saw too the equal force of grace.

The morning of the fourth day, we woke to silence. It was over. We walked outside, not ready yet to repair the damages, but just to breathe air that was still. We were exhausted, and somehow, the air felt limp as well, depleted. The winds as they swept over our island had taken something with them.

We didn't get much done those next days before we packed up and headed back to town. A little work—some siding put up, a drain for a future bathroom sink, a room rearranged for the new baby. We hiked to the top of the mountain, scouted the beaches for firewood in the skiff. It almost didn't matter what we did. The real event had happened already. Somehow we knew without saying it that nothing else mattered. We were alive, we were together, and whatever the storm had taken from us, it gave all of that back.

Leslie Leyland Fields lives in Kodiak, Alaska most of the time, where she works every summer in commercial fishing with her husband and six children, ages twenty-two to seven. She teaches in Seattle Pacific University's Master of Fine Arts program, and is the author of seven creative nonfiction books, including Surviving the Island of Grace, Out on the Deep Blue, *and* Surprise Child. *She has recently returned from nine months of travel throughout North and Central America with her family, and is studying the map for the next trip, despite her children's protests.*

DURGA YAEL BERNHARD

* * *

The Gift of Artemis

Hunting from a mother's perspective.

AN HOUR BEFORE MY ALARM WAS SET TO GO OFF, MY growling stomach and full bladder roused me from restless sleep. In the dim light of the setting moon, I could barely make out the outline of my cat curled up in the folds of my bedspread.

Squinting in the light of the refrigerator, I reached for milk and poured myself a bowl of cereal. The clock on the windowsill read 3:30 A.M. I was eight weeks pregnant and famished.

Instead of going back to bed, I switched off the alarm clock and reached into an ice chest near the door. It was full of camouflage hunting gear, safely stored away from household odors. Above the chest hung my compound bow, its quiver full of razor-sharp arrows. I pulled on insulated pants, a silk undershirt, a turtleneck, and a jacket. Over my clothes went a layer of camouflage, followed by camouflage facenet and hat. As I fastened my climbing safety harness around my waist, my cat rubbed against my legs, begging to be fed. Hastily I scooped some food into his dish, then sprayed my hands with scent eliminator. Then I took my bow down from its hook and slipped out into the clear moonlit night.

The cold November air brushed my face as I strapped my climbing treestand to my back and entered the nearby woods. Enveloped in silence, watching carefully for familiar shapes, I picked my way through the darkness. Stepping over logs and pausing whenever I felt a twig underfoot, I tried to step quietly through the dry leaves. Slowly I made my way up the mountain. The black silhouette of a young hemlock told me where to turn, and soon the land leveled off.

Twenty minutes later, I was climbing the straight trunk of a tall maple that I had picked out weeks earlier. Moving slowly and deliberately as a tree sloth, I eased my treestand up through the darkness, stopping just beneath the first large branching limb. Cautiously I settled into the treestand seat and hauled my bow up on its rope.

Fifteen feet up in the air, I breathed the predawn air and looked around. The forest was a tapestry of black trunks and interlocking branches that stood like sentinels in the dark.

It was forty-five minutes before sunrise. Scarcely an hour since my last meal, my stomach was already growling. Surrounded in the immense silence, I leaned back against the trunk of the tree and waited.

Soon the sky began to lighten in a notch between the mountains to the east. I watched as the autumn landscape, coarse as wool, slowly took shape around me. As the morning birds awakened, the forest seemed as pregnant with hidden life as my own body: I took an arrow from the quiver and clipped the nock in place on the bowstring. I sat up straight and felt my aching breasts press against my camouflage, noticeably tighter than a week ago. Preparing to draw back, I began to scan the forest floor for prey.

Time passed, and the timeless cloak of silence slowly wrapped itself around me. As I sat motionless against the great tree, I felt myself almost disappear, drawn as a single strand into the living tapestry of my surroundings. How easily this trance came over me in my dreamy first-trimester state...how quickly I found my own presence blending into the forest. A great sense of privilege came over me; this was the most peaceful part of hunting—and what most predators, both animal and human, spend most of their time doing: waiting, watching, and listening.

Again my stomach growled, interrupting the silence. A wave of nausea followed. This was not the ordinary hunger I had grown used to ignoring while out in the woods. Normally I could quell my body's cravings for hours at a time. Now there was an urgency to this hunger that I knew would drive me out of the woods within an hour or two. Already this pregnancy was making its mark upon my habits; already I was changing.

The sound of rustling leaves turned my attention to the right. It was more defined than the swish of a squirrel's tail, so familiar to all deer hunters of the northern woods. These steps came in succession, with space between that suggested the lifting of feet. Holding my breath, I waited for the deer to come into view.

The footsteps stopped and started as the two deer paused in exquisite alertness to the world around them. Ever watchful for predators, these animals of prey never failed to awe me with their fine senses. As if in slow motion, the silhouette of a doe moved through the space between the trees. A second doe followed some twenty yards behind.

The fiber optic sights on my bow had barely begun to glow. It was not yet light enough to shoot. I clipped my wrist release to the bowstring, waiting for the gaining light, hoping the deer would move within range. Would I be able to pull off the shot? Six months of preparation hung in the balance as I watched the two animals.

When the deer began to amble away I took a fawn bleat call from my pocket and released the sound once, cutting the silence with the sudden noise. The larger doe stopped, turning her ears and lifting her nose. A minute, two minutes, five minutes passed in frozen silence. Barely visible behind a tree, she raised and lowered her head. With a flick of her tail, she began to walk toward me, circling round and stopping behind a young sapling that stood between us. The deer turned broadside less than twenty yards away—well within range—but a branch, still sparsely covered with brown leaves, clearly stretched in front of her vitals. The shot would be too risky. Ready to draw back, I dared not move a muscle. My heart pounded; I could feel the blood pulsing through my swollen womb. Time vanished as I waited breathlessly for her to step out from behind the tree, hoping she would offer herself, praying for the gift of success.

Then as if a spell had been broken, the deer simply turned her white tail toward me, and walked straight away, never emerging from either side of the tree. I exhaled involuntarily and slouched back against the trunk. Within a moment, the doe's footsteps had faded into the silence, and the forest was still.

It was my last opportunity to shoot that season.

I waited another hour in my treestand, watching the sunrise turn the forest from blacks and grays to the golden hues of autumn. I considered the doe who had *not* offered herself to me on this day. Had I sought to prey upon another mother? It was too early still for the rut; she would not be pregnant yet as I was. But if she lived through this year's hunting season, she would almost certainly give birth in the spring, at the same time my own baby was due.

My cravings for protein had been steadily increasing every day. Even as my nausea and fatigue also increased, making it harder and harder to get out of bed before dawn, my drive to hunt was never greater. For me, there was no commercial meat that matched the richness and vitality of wild game. I preferred to take my meat directly from the land, rather than delegate the responsibility of killing to someone else. And even as new life spun itself into form from my own flesh and blood, there was something just as fertile, just as embryonic in the exchange of wild flesh to feed new life.

But my pregnancy had its own agenda. As with my two older children, I soon found it was not up to me what sacrifices I would make for this child. Two weeks later, a threatened miscarriage (unrelated to hunting) nearly aborted the rest of my hunting season, forcing me to stay close to home and avoid exertion. After a week of rest, I hunted from the ground only; wandering in the woods mostly on private land near a friend's house. As the weather grew colder, I exchanged bow for shotgun, venturing out for short spells before sunset, and arriving home just in time to cook dinner.

"Did you get anything?" my teenage son asked as I peeled off my gear.

"Not today."

"You smell, Mom." He waved his hand at the rank odor of my cover scent—raccoon or fox urine, depending on the terrain.

My daughter bounced into the kitchen. "What's for dinner?"

"Venison pizza," I said, pulling a package of defrosted meat from last year out of the refrigerator.

"Yum! My favorite. Well, I'm glad you won't be up late butchering tonight."

What did my children learn from watching their mother bring home meat directly from the forest? For them, it was not unusual to see blood on my clothes, bones on the kitchen counter, heart and liver soaking in the sink. Whenever a dead deer was hauled into the garage, my daughter would come and look. She crouched down to look at its lovely eyes that always turned mysteriously blue after death. In our era of mass manufacturing and food production, how many children have the experience of running their hands over the soft fur of an animal that would soon become food on the table? Always, her words would sketch out the same paradox: "I'm glad we get to eat this meat, Mom, but I wish the deer didn't have to die."

Her words echoed the age-old quandary expressed in *The Yearling*, the classic story of a boy growing up in a southern homesteading family, written in 1938 by Marjorie Kinnan Rawlings. Halfway through the book, young Jody expresses his feelings forthrightly after witnessing a kill:

> *"I hate things dyin'," Jody said.*
> *The men were silent.*
> *Penny said slowly, "Nothin's spared, son, if that be ary comfort to you."*
> *"'Taint."*
> *"Well, hit's a stone wall nobody's yit clumb over. You kin kick it and crack your head agin it and holler, but nobody'll listen and nobody'll answer."*

As Jody grows up, he learns to accept death as a natural and inevitable part of life. His father, however, does not teach Jody to harden his heart. In fact, he allows his son to take in an orphaned fawn, whom Jody learns to care for deeply even as he participates in the hunt.

The same paradox is still faced by all hunters today—all hunters, that is, who rightly respect their chosen prey. Whether hunting for sport or subsistence, whether meat is taken directly from the land or purchased in a store, the truth remains the same: one way or another, life feeds upon life. If children can be comfortable with death, if they can learn to take their place in the natural scheme of things with reverence and grace, that is a valuable lesson.

Life and death have not always presented the contradiction that we struggle intellectually to come to terms with today: in ancient mythologies, they were woven together as one. Artemis, the ancient Greek goddess of both the hunt and childbirth, is a prime example. Bearing the emblem of the crescent moon, she skillfully presides over the affairs of women. It was only natural that she should usher life both in and out— both of which were accompanied by the threat of death. Known also as "Lady of Wild Things" and "Mistress of the Animals," her ministrations were considered kind, not cruel.

Not only does the beauty of wildlife not contradict the purpose of the hunt—it is an intrinsic part of it. To me, the deer is unspeakably beautiful: its grace and agility, its quiet dignity and exquisitely fine senses always find their way into my work as an artist. The more intimately I come to know their patterns and habits, the more I am privileged with direct observation, direct contact, and direct consumption of their flesh, the more reverence I feel for these incredible wild creatures. Every kill is a priceless gift of both experience and nourishment. Apart from childbirth itself, I could not think of a greater blessing, or a more immediate way to participate in the process of life and death.

The blessings extend far beyond the actual hunt, too. From its conception, this fetus was growing on the meat of not only deer, but black bear—shot in the backwoods of Maine just weeks before the pregnancy began—and wild turkey as well. Sometimes, a fellow hunter would give us pheasant, or extra venison in a season without success—an experience that almost every hunter has to face. Occasionally I would even take a fresh road kill. More often than not, the deer was killed by a blow to the head; I could not bear to let so much undamaged meat go to waste. One way or another, our family frequently had some kind of wild meat on the table. In our area, away from the pesticides of orchards and farms, the meat was completely organic. Wild animals, especially browsers, live on an incredible variety of wild plants, nuts, berries, insects, barks, and roots. They are hardier, leaner, and possess greater strength and vitality than domestic animals. All of this translates into the meat. And unlike animals raised in captivity for slaughter, hunted prey live wild and free in their natural state—provided they are taken by a skillful hunter—until the moment of death.

The hunt also brings home other bounty: wild plants for both food and medicine, foraged while scouting and tracking; ideas and inspiration for paintings; photographs taken during every season; and a sense of connection and intimacy with the surrounding mountains that roots us deeply to our environment and gives an immediate sense of our place in the web of life.

All of this is naturally understood by my children, and at the same time seems to foster respect in them for wildlife. Although they haven't yet participated directly in the hunt, they are deeply affected by it. Through the seasons, they are witness to endless target practice, scouting and planning, and final sighting in and preparations, followed by the excitement of opening day. Later, with a little luck, they see the whole process of gutting and skinning, quartering, butchering, and finally the cooking of game into meals. They share the bounty of the season and through the winter, sleep with deer pelts on their beds. They watch paintings come to life that memorialize animals sighted, animals taken, and animals let go. My daughter, with her more sensitive nature, seems to mourn the loss of beauty in the sacrifice of every innocent creature, even as she is equally fascinated and amazed. The inevitably two-sided nature of hunting touches her very deeply. My son, for his part, accepts the sacrifice of life more readily and seems more interested in the nuts-and-bolts process. The aero-dynamics of arrow trajectory and bullet drop, mastering aim under pressure, and the critical monitoring of wind direction and scent all fascinate him. I try to teach my children that hunting is both a challenge and a sacrament; both modern and poetic; an opportunity for both skill and inspiration—and above all, for communion with the natural world we live in.

That world includes all the demands and responsibilities that every mother has to juggle in order to pursue *any* passion. My attempts to weave hunting into my busy work and home life are not always successful. Even though it puts meat on the table, hunting often has to take a back seat to our family's needs. If hunting is truly meant to nourish my children, then it will have to serve their priorities, too—and take its place beside school plays, music lessons, baseball practice, and homework.

With the coming of a third baby, an entire hunting season will probably have to be sacrificed for the sake of my child. But the infant, born in the time when the does birth their fawns, will be laid on the most beautiful pelt of a black bear, and will grow up with her little fingers close to the pulse of life and death. To whatever degree hunting finds its way into my life and the lives of my children, it all seems worth it.

Durga Yael Bernhard is the author and illustrator of numerous children's books, including fiction and non-fiction, natural science titles, and multicultural folktales. She lives in the Catskill Mountains of New York with her family.

BERNADETTE MURPHY

* * *

We'll Do Whitney, Right?

A mother and son skirt the precipice
of growing up and moving on.

WHEN I SLIPPED ON THE POLISHED ROCKS ALONGSIDE Sequoia National Park's Mehrten Creek, I slammed one hip against granite and hung onto the wiry limbs of an insubstantial bush lest I fall into the rushing flow of snowmelt beside me. I began to wonder whether this two-day High Sierra backpacking trip I'd undertaken with my sixteen-year-old son, Jarrod, was such a good idea. Though we've camped in the western Sierras every summer since he was an infant, and spent an occasional winter snowshoeing there too, backpacking was a whole new thing—for both of us.

Jarrod had been asking to backpack for years, though I kept waiting until there was some kind of adult to show us how. Then one day a friend pointed out that I was an adult. I could do this.

We were only five or so miles into our outing, and I was having second and third thoughts. Carrying a thirty-pound pack while walking even gradually uphill was much harder and more painful than I'd expected. Balancing it across a dashing tumult of water, near impossible. My feet were killing me.

I thought my boots were broken in but realized too late that they were about half a size too small. My tailbone felt raw from the pack's friction, and I swore my collarbones were bruised.

Jarrod helped me up from the slick rocks and we plotted how we might yet get across the riotous creek. I changed my hiking boots for Teva sandals, threw my pack to the other side, and waded through the glacial water, screaming with relief and feet-numbness once I breached the opposite shore. Jarrod tossed over his pack next and I lobbed him my sandals, five sizes too small, which he wedged onto his feet and then plowed through, shrieking with the cold.

We'd left Jarrod's younger siblings and dad back at the Lodgepole campground in the park and had taken off at 7 A.M. along the High Sierra Trail. Though Dad is a willing car camper, he's not exactly an avid outdoorsman; he had no interest in joining our expedition. Our original plan had been to go to Pear Lake at the alpine level, a breathtaking area we'd visited previous years on day hikes, but that path, along with just about every other choice in the region, was closed due to late-season snow and ice. The only reasonable trail available, the ranger in the Wilderness Office had told us when we'd applied for our permit, was the High Sierra Trail, one we'd never before hiked. "Use caution with the high and fast creek crossings," she'd noted on the permit.

We'd set out with a map and compass in my pocket, sleeping bag and food in our packs. If we stayed on this trail long enough—seventy-one miles—we'd eventually make it to Mt. Whitney. That's what Jarrod would have liked for this outing, he being sixteen, but I'd talked him into a more reasonable first experience: a hike to Bear Paw Meadow, some eleven-plus miles along the well-marked trail, and then back again.

"But in September," Jarrod kept announcing as we made our way, snow-topped peaks to our right and massive pines to our left, "we'll do Whitney, right?"

A friend of ours, a park ranger, had mentioned that he'd have some time off in late September and that maybe he'd be available to make the ten-day-plus outing with us.

"September, right?" Jarrod asked again.

My son sported Converse All Stars on his feet. At first, I'd thought he was foolish not to wear boots, but now I discarded all I'd learned from backpacking books and followed his lead, refusing to put my own boots back on after the water crossing and making the rest of the trek in sandals. My feet praised this decision every step of the way.

We'd set out on the summer solstice. After today, the sun's journey across the sky would begin to shorten, day by day. I was in the same position with my son. My influence over him, the central location I'd long held in his life, was about to shift. The day we would return from the Sierras, in fact, he'd start packing for a six-week stay in Michigan to study music, his first major venture away from home. Away from me. In two years, he'd be packing for college. As he walked the path ahead of me, his poorly attached sleeping bag at the bottom of his pack swayed with each step, looking for all the world like a saggy, overloaded diaper.

The words of Kahlil Gibran's "On Children" came to mind: "You may give them your love but not your thoughts. For they have their own thoughts. You may house their bodies but not their souls, for their souls dwell in the house of to-morrow, which you cannot visit, even in your dreams."

We continued on, walking for hours, making slow progress. We passed a mother grouse, shepherding her little ball-of-fluff babies along a rocky ledge. (Jarrod identified the fowl species, which I initially thought might be quail; he knows his birds much better than I.) A small bear, perhaps a yearling, rustled by a mile or so later, taking scant notice of us. At a high elevation, a striped red, yellow, and black snake startled us on the trail, passing within inches of Jarrod's Converse. "Red to yellow, kill a fellow," he calmly recited the saying he'd learned to tell a non-venomous king snake from its poisonous look-alike, the coral snake. "Red to black, venom lack." The snake's red stripes, we'd noticed, were next to the black ones. "It's O.K., Mom," he reassured me. "It's fine."

This is what it's all about, I thought. Teaching the next generation to see the wonders of nature, and then sitting back to learn from them when their knowledge surpasses our own.

What seemed like miles and miles later, we hit snow and dropped to our knees to make snow cones (unflavored, of course) and rejoiced in the unexpected refreshment. Near 4 P.M., bone tired, we made camp. Jarrod pitched the tent as I tried to figure out how to work the "Camp Heat" thing we'd purchased in lieu of a backpacking stove. No luck. We made a fire instead and put our camp kettle right next to the burning embers to boil water for dinner and drinking water for the next day. As the daylight began to change, we doused the flames and headed up a rocky peak to watch the sun's goodbye passage on this, the last gloriously long day of the year.

Jarrod and I sat on a massive outcropping facing the snow-encrusted Western Divide as the sun sank behind us, painting the ice and rocks purple and pink. We spoke little, waiting for the moon to rise. It took longer than I'd expected, but once risen, lit up the entire forest. I reached up and mussed his hair.

Back in our tent during the night, my hulking son asleep next to me, I watched that ridiculously bright moon through the bug netting, the pine trees swaying above. A sound like horses galloping made my chest tighten, until two deer passed a hair's breadth from where we lay. I may not have taught him

all he'll need to navigate his life, but I've taught him enough
to get us this far.

The next day, sore and achy, we were ready to move on. We
hiked homeward, and when tiredness overtook us, we shouted
lines of the "Jabberwocky"—"O frabjous day! Callooh!
Callay!"—and then we quieted and hiked in silence, passing
the trail mix back and forth.

"But in September," Jarrod tried not to betray his own exhaustion, "we'll do Whitney, right?"

"We'll see," I told him. I didn't have any better answer than
that.

For all I know, Whitney may be a part of his future alone,
the house of tomorrow where his soul dwells—that place I
will never visit, not even in my dreams. Or at least, not until I
buy boots that fit.

*Bernadette Murphy is the author of three narrative nonfiction books,
including* Zen and the Art of Knitting *and* The Tao Gals'
Guide to Real Estate. *She teaches creative writing in the MFA
program at Antioch University and climbed Mt. Whitney in October
2009 with her son Jarrod.*

⋆ ⋆ ⋆

Quality Time
Below Ground

*In the depths of a cave, teenage daughters may actually
admit they don't know everything.*

RIS AND PEANUT PAUSED AT THE EDGE OF THE WOODS,
their flashlight beams darting like anxious fireflies. The beams
barely pierced the dark, thick underbrush of the Kentucky
woods. "So the cave's back there somewhere?" I could hear
the tension in Ris's voice. Peanut stood beside her, her brow
crinkled with uncertainty.

"Don't worry," I told them. "Just stay behind me."

We picked our way a short distance into the woods, watching for any signs of movement in the underbrush. They were
so absorbed in watching for snakes that they ran into me when
I stopped.

"What is it?" Ris squeaked. "A snake?"

"No. We're here." Their flashlight beams darted aimlessly
again. "Down here." I pointed to a hole in the ground hidden
by thick undergrowth and mossy leaves.

The apprehension in their faces gave me second thoughts.
Our family time was nearly nonexistent now that our girls
were teenagers. They preferred to spend their time holed up
in their rooms or hanging out at the mall. So when they expressed an interest in joining our caving group, we jumped at

the opportunity. Maybe we shouldn't have. Maybe they weren't ready for caving yet. But how much time did we really have left? Ris was already in high school, Peanut would be soon. How many more caving opportunities did we have left before they went off to college and lives of their own?

"Are you sure you want to do this?" I asked while we waited for my uncle to go in first. They both nodded. "O.K. Stay behind me and go slow. Keep your hands out of the cracks—the snakes like to hide in them." I sat down, my nose filled with the smell of crushed leaves and wet earth. I shined my flashlight into the moss-covered cracks as I slid slowly down the 45-degree tunnel. At the bottom, I turned and looked up. Both girls were leaning over the hole, peering down at me. They looked impressed. "Your turn," I called up to them.

They slid carefully down the tunnel and joined me—they were inside their first cave. They took a moment to soak it all in: the distant sound of dripping water, the strange formations like giant, twisted fingers reaching from the floor, the jagged stalactites hanging like teeth from the ceiling. Even the temperature was an adjustment: the night outside had been 95 degrees. Inside the cave, it was 58 degrees.

"Cool," they said in unison.

I chuckled. "Just wait. It gets better."

My uncle had moved ahead, looking for other tunnels, and the girls started to follow him. "Not so fast," I said. "First rule of caving is to stay together. He's scouting, so he's allowed to wander off. But we have to wait here for the others."

They shined their flashlights around while we waited and finally noticed the paw prints on the floor. "Whose dog has been down here?" Ris asked.

"Nobody's dog. This is a coyote den. If you'd pulled back the weeds by the entrance, you would have seen their tracks in the mud."

They clustered closer to me, their flashlights darting around. "Coyotes?"

"It's all right. They're out hunting for the night and they won't come back while we're here."

"Are you ready?" My mother and the rest of the group had made it into the chamber and were ready to go deeper.

I turned to look at the girls. Their eyes were shining with an awe and excitement that I hadn't seen since they entered their sullen, hard-to-impress teen years. "Are we?" I asked them.

"Are we ever!"

We crossed to the far end of the chamber to where a tunnel led down to the next level. The girls lined up behind me in the greasy, red-clay mud. "Be careful," I warned them. "This tunnel ends in a crack about a foot wide, but about fifty feet deep. You'll need to step over it. There's a ledge on the other side of the crack, and that's where we'll be going."

We slid carefully down the tunnel. At the end, the girls shined their flashlights down the crack. The beams didn't even come close to reaching the bottom. Then we sat down on the ledge and waited for everyone else to join us. My father was the last one down and immediately he ducked down the crack. My daughters gasped.

"It's O.K.; he's been down the crack before. Now turn off your lights while we wait for him to scout ahead."

They hesitated.

"You want to conserve the batteries as much as possible— you don't want your light going out when you're deep in the cave. Just sit still and you'll be O.K. Besides, you haven't seen real darkness until you've seen the darkness of being a quarter mile underground."

That sold them. They shut off their flashlights and we were pitched into absolute darkness. I felt two teens snuggle closer to me—whether for warmth or comfort, I couldn't be sure.

We sat in the darkness, our eyes useless, and let our ears take over. Somewhere in the distance, water was rushing.

I felt a breeze snap past my face. Ris's light flicked on.

"What was that?" Something darted past her beam, too fast for her to make out.

"Relax. Grandpa's scared up some bats."

They fired off a barrage of questions.

"Do they bite?"

"Are they vampire bats?"

"Will they get tangled in our hair?"

"Do they have rabies?"

"Do they have fleas?"

I tried to keep up. "They don't bite unless provoked. These are insect-eating bats, not blood-drinking bats. The tangle-in-the-hair thing is mainly a myth; they're no more likely to get tangled in your hair than a robin or sparrow might. Sometimes they do carry rabies, so I wouldn't try petting one. Sometimes they have fleas…or lice."

"Sick," Ris said. "They're rats with wings!"

"No, they're not pests, they're good. They eat a ton of insects." Their faces were still twisted in disgust. "Turn off your lights. I want to show you something."

They turned off their lights. After a few minutes passed, I told them to turn their flashlights back on and point the beams upward. They swirled their beams around the low-hanging ceiling.

"Look." I pointed to a bat hanging in one of the crevasses. "Ewww!"

"No, *really* look at him," I said, standing up, my face less than a foot from the bat. "Look how cute and fuzzy his little face is."

They stood and cautiously moved closer. The bat swiveled his velvety ears, his tiny nose twitching.

"Oh! He's shivering," Ris said.

I smiled. "He's scared. We're so much bigger than he is, he's probably wondering if we're going to eat him."

"Aw, can we take him home?" Peanut asked.

"No way," I laughed. "He's a little rat with wings!"

Just then, my father poked his head back out of the crack and broke the bad news that it had opened up too much for us to go down. So we left the little bat and climbed back up the mud chute. Half an hour later we were deep in a gravel chute, surrounded by rock waterfalls and crystal clear pools. The girls stopped to look at some white, blind crayfish. As Ris tried to catch one, a drip of water plunked onto her head and she yelped in surprise.

"It gets worse. Reach up and feel your hair."

She reached up. "Gross! It feels crunchy!"

"This water contains dissolved minerals. As the water moves through the cave, the minerals are deposited. Every drip has the potential to build stalagmites, including the drop that dripped in your hair."

"So if I sat still long enough, would it turn me into rock?"

"No. The depositing takes hundreds, maybe thousands of years to build anything." I shined my light on the formation closest to us. It looked like a frozen waterfall, twenty feet high and fifteen feet wide, solid rock. "Drip by drip, you can imagine how long it took to create this."

We stepped ahead to a hole in the floor, a tunnel to the next level. We slid down it, our feet slipping in the wet grit. At the end of the tunnel was a large room filled with fallen rock. Five tunnels led out of it.

"Which way do we go?" Ris asked.

"We'll need to split up," my father said. "In groups of two and three, each group taking a tunnel. I'll stay here and watch over all the groups."

Ris volunteered to go with her dad, Peanut wanted to come with me. I let Peanut choose our tunnel and we started our team exploration.

"It's so dark," she whispered. The tunnel was just tall enough for us to stand up in, the walls solid rock worn smooth by years of water.

"It's no darker than anyplace else. What's really getting to you is the isolation. We're probably a quarter mile underground, completely surrounded by rock. If you wanted to be completely and utterly alone, this is where you'd want to be."

She mulled this over for a minute. Complete and utter isolation holds a lot of appeal for a teenager. But then she must have considered the drawbacks. "What do we do if we run into a bear?"

"Bears don't like to go really deep in a cave, so listen for crickets. If you hear crickets, then our tunnel opens out on the surface. Near the surface is where the wild things will be."

Up ahead, there was a hole punched in our tunnel wall. We stopped beside it and flashed our beams downward, where another tunnel ran below us.

"So do we go down there?"

"No. We don't go off our main track, or else we might get confused about which way is the way back. We wait until we can explore it as a group.

We continued on. We could no longer hear the others; the only sound was our breathing. Our tunnel curved and forked into three tunnels.

"Now what?" Peanut asked.

"Now you wait here," I said.

"I want to go!"

"No. You're job is to stay here so I know where to come back to. You just sit here at the junction."

She waved her flashlight around. "But I'll be alone."

"You'll be all right, I won't be far away. And this time you can leave your light on." I knew it would be a good test of her cave-readiness. Sitting alone was something almost everyone had to do at some point in the exploration—it was what my father was doing at the same moment, while he waited for the rest of us to finish our small team explorations. But I also didn't want to leave her alone for too long or stray very far away from her, so I explored the first two tunnels as quickly as I could: one continued on and would have to be explored later; the second dead-ended at a rock wall.

The third tunnel started out with smooth, water-worn walls, tall enough that I could walk in. But soon I was walking hunched over, gravel crunching beneath my feet. Then the ceiling dropped and I had to crawl through the gravel, the rocks digging into my knees and elbows. Then the ceiling dropped more and the floor turned to sand.

"Are you O.K.?" Peanut's voice was surprisingly calm.

I paused and sucked in a deep breath of the cold, wet air. "I'm fine. I'm almost ready to turn around."

I scooted forward on my belly. It looked like the tunnel ended in a sand wall, but as I drew closer I could see that the tunnel was only *almost* clogged with sand. There was a tiny opening, but I couldn't risk crawling through it alone. I called Peanut to join me and waited patiently as she "ouched" and "oofed" her way through the biting gravel.

She was grinning from ear to ear. "That was cool!"

"I'm going to crawl through. You wait right here."

"What? You can't get through that hole."

"I can at least get in enough to see what's behind it. If I get stuck, though, you're going to have to drag me back out by my feet."

She looked skeptical. I wormed my way through, the wet sand pushing down the neck of my shirt. Past the sand "dam," the tunnel went on for quite a distance, finally curving away out of sight.

I backed out of the hole. "We aren't going to be able to explore that one. Grandma isn't going to want to crawl a mile on her belly."

"Can I look?" she asked. She wiggled her way until only her legs and butt were left on my side. "We could make it!"

I laughed. "Yeah, but Grandma can't. Maybe next time."

She wiggled back out and stopped to catch her breath. "That was cool!" She slid up her sleeve and pointed her flashlight at the back of her arm. I could see blood welled up in little dots where the sand had scoured her skin.

"We'll get some antiseptic on those when we get back home."

She grinned. "I hope they scar. These are cave wounds, I want to keep them forever!" Was this really the same girl who wouldn't leave her house without makeup? Who thought one zit was the end of the world? And now she was begging for scar tissue!

After four hours exploring the cave, we decided to call it a night.

"I want to see more. We should keep going," Ris said.

"Nope. Another cave rule: know when to stop. If you go to the point of exhaustion, you might not be able to make it back out. We'll save the rest for next time."

Mud-covered and wet, we trudged out of the cave and piled back into the truck. As we rode down the country roads, we tilted our heads back and stared into the inky bits of sky visible through the thick canopy of trees.

"So many stars," Ris murmured. "We never see this many stars in the backyard."

The pickup increased speed, the wind whipped our hair in our faces. The temperature had dropped to the mid-70s, but in the back of the pickup, cave-soaked and bone weary, it was cold. My two teens snuggled close against me and put my arms around them. My husband and I shared a knowing smile. So much good comes out of a night of caving: science lessons; lessons about the importance of rules, of teamwork; lessons about respecting and caring for the natural world; lessons about courage and self-reliance. But even if none of that applied, it would still be worthwhile, just for the family time we shared…and riding in the back of a pickup with my two happy girls snuggled at my side and a sky full of stars overhead.

Brenda Kezar is a writer and home-schooling mom living in North Dakota. She and her husband have three daughters, and share their home with two dogs, multiple cats, and an assortment of small animals. Between hairballs, she writes every chance she gets.

DOUG LEIER

I Want My Duckies Back

Nothing Dad could say or do while stuck in the mud
would change his two-year-old mind.

ABOUT THE TIME JOE SLURPED THE LAST SIP OF CHOCOLATE milk from the bottom of the mug, we rolled to a stop a few hundred yards from the marsh where our duck hunt would take place. It only took a few minutes to unload gear and put on my waders. We were set. I had my gun, shells, and decoy bag. Joe had his toy gun and binoculars. Everything going as planned, we headed out across the grass heading into the marsh.

As I walked, I packed down the tall grass to make a path for my soon-to-be three-year-old. I realized that, in his eyes, we may as well have been cutting a trail through a jungle. After each step I waited for him to climb up and over the mounds of matted-down grass. Thankfully we were yards, not miles, from our destination. I knew that with a youngster the journey itself might mark the end of our hunt.

If he was too tired to make it down to the shore, he'd soon be ready to head home. I've found that a cardinal rule of introducing kids to the outdoors is to leave before they're ready to go, so as to keep them wanting more. At a minimum, once they verbalize "Can we go now?" or anything close to it, you'd better employ your exit strategy.

That day I was fortunate. As we reached the open shoreline, the thrill of scaling each mountain of packed grass was still holding Joe's attention. The virtual sea of grass opened wide to the marsh, flush with ducks, coots, cattails, and shore birds. Joe's eyes glimmered with anticipation of the next obstacle his able mind and body would conquer on this toddler expedition.

I plopped the decoy bag and equipment on a dry spot a yard from the exposed mud flat and sat down to relate how this next part of the hunt would need to play out. I explained that I'd venture out into the slough and set out the decoys while he hunkered down on shore with his binoculars and checked out all the different birds in the area.

After securing my equipment I began trudging through the mud. A stretch of five yards was more like a mile as the muck was knee-deep and sucked my waders from my feet. A quick backward glance assured me that Joe was still perched upon the gear observing the flight of avocets and cormorants. At this point I don't think he realized exactly what I was doing, but he was content with the fact that Dad was still within sight. I hollered an update every minute or so— "There's a drake mallard"—followed by a splash as I tossed the decoy into place.

Battling back through the mud toward shore, I told Joe that I was all done placing decoys, ready to hunker down for our hunt. And what did he say?

"I want my duckies back!"

I mulled this over, and my heart started shuddering. What could I say? Nothing. I didn't say a word, maybe in a way hoping my lack of acknowledgment would distract him long enough to forget. But this was a two-year-old; I was in deep.

I'd tossed every decoy out and couldn't reach even one to give him. His plea rang out again, "I want my duckies back!"

He rose from the pile of gear, and I struggled to reach him. "Joe, stay there. We'll get them in a little bit."

Even as I spoke, I realized the futility of asking a toddler to stay while having no means of restraining him.

He was going to rescue the ducks, and nothing I could say or do while stuck in the mud would change his mind.

He took a step and I winced, hollering, "Joe, I'm almost there!" and knowing full well I was about three minutes from reaching him. He advanced again, and his little red boots were baptized with mud. I yelled louder, but he was undaunted. One more step and the mud won. Boots, coveralls, hands, face—mud from head to toe.

I knew at that exact moment that our duck hunting was done for the day. Not even the prospect of bringing home a duck—or limit of ducks—was going to convince Joe to stick it out in his condition. He wanted to be clean, wanted Mom. Using a piece of bark like a trawl, I scraped off the sticky mire and calmed him by promising I'd go out and get his duckies back. And so, mere minutes after we'd arrived for the hunt, we were staging our exit from the marsh.

After this debacle Joe had no desire to master the mountains of cattails and grass. He wanted to go back to the car, and I wanted to get him there quick. I packed up the gear and somehow managed to include him on my shoulders as I set off with the lyrics "He ain't heavy, he's my *son*" humming through my mind. A smile crept across my face feeling Joe holding onto my neck with all his might.

With a stack of wet wipes, I got Joe cleaned up enough for the ride. By the time I'd turned down the gravel road toward home, he was happily fist-deep in a bag of Cheetos, sipping on a juice box. So what if we didn't have any ducks to show for our efforts? We bagged a darn good story to tell Mom.

Doug Leier is a biologist for the North Dakota Game and Fish Department in West Fargo. He and wife Michelle, son Joseph, and daughters Kaitlyn and Grace spend every waking minute outdoors, or wishing they were on the other side of the window.

CINDY ROSS

* * *

A Windstorm on the Continental Divide

A gusty brush with danger reminds a family
what it means to be alive.

I'M IN MONTANA'S ROCKIES WALKING ON THE BACKBONE of the continent with my family and a few friends. We are hiking a 500-mile stretch of the 3,100-mile National Scenic Continental Divide Trail. While my husband Todd and I walk, our three-year-old son, Bryce, and five-year-old daughter, Sierra, cover most of the ground on the backs of their llamas. Every year, we trailer our llamas from Pennsylvania to spend the summer hiking the Divide trail, gradually making our way south from Canada to Mexico.

Today, the wind blows unceasingly, flinging my hair in my eyes and across my face. My visor sails down the mountainside with me in chase, and wind sucks the saliva from my mouth when I try to yell to one of the kids. It's the kind of wind that makes me want to huddle under a bush, crouch low, and stay put. It's the kind of wind that makes me anxious, because I know we're on the borderline this time.

Todd and I have been in 100 mph gusts on top of Mount Washington in New Hampshire, and it was mighty scary. It literally picked us off our feet and dropped us yards away. But it was just the two of us then. We tend to push ourselves pretty close to the edge of what we think we can handle. But it's a different story when you have your babes along in the wilderness. And as light as they are...

As parents, we're responsible for our children's well-being, and Todd and I take that charge seriously. But, for us, their well-being means much more than keeping them physically safe. It also means making sure Bryce and Sierra spend time in the natural world and are exposed to new challenges. But at times like these, I wonder if we're exposing them to too much of a challenge. I know we can all handle this, but what if the wind gets worse? How much fear is too much? I've never been good at hiding worry or doubt from my children. Couple that with perceptive kids, and there aren't many secrets between us.

About the time the wind picks up, the children pick up on their parents' tension. It's in the air, like electricity.

"Daddy's going to put you in the backpack," Todd says to Bryce, who is light enough to be blown off his llama's saddle. But when Todd puts Bryce in the pack, the wind immediately unsnaps the rain awning. The wind's force holds the awning and all the pack's loose straps horizontal. Todd grabs the wool pad Bryce sits on before it blows away.

Sierra looks at me, her face full of concern. I try to console her. "We'll be O.K., honey. We're going to go down now. The wind should die down as we lose elevation."

But this isn't what happens. The lower we drop into the saddle, the swifter the wind becomes. "Get off your llama, Sierra, and hold my hands," I tell her. I place her directly in front of me, so as the wind pushes her, she can lean into my body. I grip both her hands and her llama, Berrick's, lead rope.

Down below, bathed in deceiving sunlight, the lowlands look inviting. In the canyon to my left, a herd of nearly one hundred elk run across the open flat. Sierra and I stand and watch them, as the rest of our group catches up. "The smaller ones are calves," I tell Sierra, who is in love with all animals.

"Look at those big ones, Mommy," she points out. "Look at their antlers!"

They are all running at the same speed, and we wonder what has spooked them. We frequently see herds of elk at these heights on the Divide, but with so little cover, we never get very close to them.

"I wish I were down there with the elk, Mommy," Sierra muses. "It looks so safe."

I swallow hard and nod in agreement, then direct my attention back to the problem at hand. We soon discover that the saddle ahead is acting as a wind tunnel, gathering the wind up the valley and funneling it like a freight train right over the Divide. Todd and I glance at one another, checking in on each other's anxiety. His eyes show alarm.

The lower we descend and the closer we get to the saddle, the more trouble we have standing up. We take each step consciously, slowly, placing one foot down and locking the knee before lifting the other foot. We have to be careful not to lose balance. I grasp Sierra's hands tightly and hold her arms out and up. We move as one mass.

Just as we approach the saddle, the wind shifts and hits us broadside, driving us both to the ground. We lie there in the dirt, stunned by the wind's strength. Sierra is cradled safely in my arms, but her llama is in trouble. I clutch tightly to his rope, as he thrashes and pulls against it. When I push myself up, I see that the wind has blown off his saddle and panniers, and the whole mess is dangling under his belly. He's going wild, trying to get it off. He stomps around, bumping into Sierra and me with his soft padded feet; scaring us more than hurting us. But I can't let go. He'd take off in a fury, get more tangled and surely hurt himself. We scream out for help, hoping Todd and our friends are nearby and can help.

Todd is about ten yards away, scrambling to get up, but he can't hear us over the wind's fury. I wave until I get his attention. Finally, he sees me and ties up his packstring of llamas to a dwarf shrub. But I see right away that he doesn't know what to do with Bryce. He's probably afraid to put him down on the ground and wouldn't leave him alone. He waits until our friend Bob Riley finally comes around the bend and hears my cries.

Bob takes the llama from me and yells, "Crawl over to Todd." We follow him and the llama to the backside of the mountain, where the wind is calmer.

We are all shaken. We gather together and decide we cannot go on. With miles of exposed trail on the long ridge ahead of us, we know it's not safe with the kids. Turning back isn't an attractive alternative either. It means making a long detour around the ridge and then hiking hard to get back on schedule. But there's no doubt.

Todd and Bob decide to crawl around the backside of the mountain, taking the llamas, one by one, to the wooded saddle where we'll make our way down. Then they'll come back for us. Our friend Bruce will stay with the kids and me.

We watch them snake through the stunted evergreens. Bryce begins to cry as his father fades into the distance. "I couldn't breathe, Mommy," he sputters. "The wind wouldn't let me breathe."

I feel my daughter tug on my jacket, and I look down into her big brown eyes filled with tears, "Are we going to be O.K., Mommy?"

I hesitate for a moment, as thoughts race through my mind: *What are we doing out here with these little ones? What are we putting them through?*

Given that we're out here for many weeks every year, we're bound to encounter something scary sooner or later. Challenging weather is just part of being in the wilderness. But knowing that doesn't make it easier. "Don't worry, honey," I say, without conviction. "We're going to be O.K. You'll see." We shove handfuls of peanut M&Ms in our mouths for energy.

The wind bites into us as we sit on the bare ground and wait. Now that we've stopped moving, we all begin to shiver, a combination of cold and fear. Bryce sniffs, trying to control his tears and stop his runny nose. When I go to wipe it, I am amazed at the depth and clarity of his blue eyes, always exaggerated when he's been crying. I slide the backpack raincovers over the kids' bodies, providing an extra layer, and snap up their backs. Bruce and I zip up our jackets and tighten our hoods to a small hole around our faces. We hold the children in our arms, trying to stop their shivering and our own.

"Do you want to say a prayer?" I ask.

They both nod their heads, yes.

We hold hands and I blurt out a few lines, asking God to keep us safe. Moments later, a huge rainbow appears in front of us, arching across the valley. We stare in disbelief, for it hasn't even been raining here.

"That's God answering our prayers," I tell the kids, my own eyes filling with tears. "He's letting us know we'll be O.K."

This sets Bryce off asking a whole string of questions. "Where is God? Is He in the clouds? Do you think He's in the rainbow? Is He in the wind?"

Amused by his tumble of questions, I tell him that God doesn't have boundaries like we do, and He's not too easy to explain. "God's sort of like when you feel love," I say, "like a warm feeling inside and outside. Kind of like the sun."

My thoughts trail back to my own childhood, and how my strict Catholic father criticized me for missing Mass when I was a young woman hiking the Appalachian Trail. And I re-member how I told him, "I don't have to go to church to find God, Dad!" I think that lesson is hitting home with my kids today, better than a whole summer's worth of Bible school lessons.

In a few minutes the rainbow fades, and we're all quieted and calmed. When the men return, we begin to contour around the knoll. With the wind calmer here, my children hike ahead of me in their colorful rain gear, glancing back from time to time to give their mother a big smile, letting me know everything is all right with their world once again. Now I feel warm inside.

We descend off the open ridge, and part of me feels cheated, knowing I'll probably never see that gorgeous stretch of high mountain trail again. And tomorrow we face a long road-walk around the mountain. As we enter the sheltered meadow, three elk trot out into the open, stopping us in our tracks. Two more, then another pair follow. We hear their high-pitched warning whistle that sounds like a bird, and the llamas' ears bend forward. We all look at each other, smiling wide grins.

My kids, like their parents, love encountering wild animals. The closer we move in their direction, the more elk we spook. The herd suddenly decides the route in front of us is the way to safety, and about eighty animals thunder by, mostly cows and calves. The elk are so close we can see the glint in their eyes. We are silent, stunned, amazed as they race past us.

Sierra and Bryce chatter excitedly about being so close to "the big elk." Even at their age, they know what real adven-ture is. Sierra would rather traipse along the top of the Continental Divide, looking for elk herds among the shadows of mountain meadows, than go to the zoo. Neither have been to Disneyland, and they may just have to wait until they are old enough to get there by themselves.

A half-mile farther, we come to a beautiful grassy area. Tall green stalks sway in the wind. From their vantage point on the llamas' backs, the kids spot oval-shaped areas where the grass is flattened. They hop off their llamas, and we all stretch out in the sun where the elk had bedded minutes before. "Their beds are still warm, Mama!" shouts Bryce.

I feel tremendous peace and contentment, lying in the elk bed. It isn't until this moment, in the warm sun of the meadow, that I finally relax enough to realize we are safe. After our long tense journey, we are all here and all O.K. I feel like we've been given a great gift. Had we not been blown off that ridge, we would have missed the grand show the elk put on for us, and we wouldn't be lying here in this wild elk bedroom together.

I'm overcome with gratitude for my fellow adventurers and for our children who are such troopers. I go around and give each of them a hug. When I hold Bryce in my arms, he blurts out, "I thought we were going to die!"

"Oh no," our friend Bob replies. "This is really living. Yes, sir. We know we are alive on a day like this."

For the past thirty years, Cindy Ross has found peace, happiness, and a sublime sense of contentment while walking and cycling the endless trails that are sewn into the fabric of the North American continent. Her sixth and latest book, Scraping Heaven: A Family's Journey Along the Continental Divide, *is the rousing adventure of a family's five-summer, 3,100-mile trek over the rooftop of North America. Cindy's current passion is the importance of educating children about the natural world. She is working on a new book in which she will share expertise gleaned from twenty years of mothering as an outdoor adventurer.*

MARTHA MOLNAR

Unmapped Days

Mother and daughter abandon the beaten path.

WE PACK ONLY AS MUCH AS WE NEED FOR ONE NIGHT. On the cool blacktop in the parking lot, we lay out all our gear, just as we've seen it in hiking magazines: stove, headlamp, extra socks, rain jacket, food carefully doled out for each modest meal. Apples, bought at a farmers' market along the Oregon coast, weigh down our pockets.

It's a steep climb to the top of the ridge, and our backs and legs are unaccustomed to the weight of our packs. After four rambling hours, we're at the summit. My daughter, Daniela, and I stand transfixed, feeling tiny under the spreading canopy of giants, caught in unexpected splendor. A single hollowed-out trunk is large enough to offer shelter for two. Far below, the Pacific is silent, stretched out taut, iridescent. A yawning white beach lies empty of people. On the other side is a perfectly round lake, an eye as unruffled and iris blue as my daughter's, as thickly fringed with forest as hers is with lashes.

We look at each other, utter wordless sounds, and dance a little jig. We have come for the shock of the newly beautiful, the discovery of a landscape different from the familiar

gentleness of the Northeast, and, above all, the thrill of finding it ourselves.

Two weeks ago, immediately following high-school grad-
uation, Daniela willfully put thousands of miles between herself and everything familiar, leaving her suburban New York
friends to search for gainful summer employment, and strik-
ing out alone across the continent. After four glorious days
and five sleepless nights aboard an Amtrak train, she arrived in
San Francisco with the happy prospect of a few more days
alone before I, her frantic mother, could join her.

Her teenage angst, a simmering anger at a terribly imper-
fect world, seemed to have subsided by the time we met up.
The world's iniquities appeared remote without regular newspapers and National Public Radio news. As we headed north
from San Francisco, the scenery along Highway 1 became pro-
gressively wilder. Our escapes from the car took us mostly to
state and national parks, still silent and empty in early June. The
ravaged land we had expected appeared amazingly unspoiled,
the clearcuts invisible, the pollution scattered by ocean breezes.

Lost in the exhilaration of the new, my "so annoying" parenting became less so. While at home my concerns about my
wild daughter's safety seemed so unfounded to her, she was
forced to share some of my misgivings here in the wild.
Conversations at home consisted of low-level debates, with
me maintaining a staunch realism in the face of her untried
idealism. But in the unbounded space of open air, our talks
flowed easily, focused on each day's simple decisions and
shared enjoyment: where to stop for a scenic lunch, in which
direction to start the circular hike, whether the firs appeared
black against the blue or a very deep green. Our similar sense
of humor, our equal willingness to take on physical challenges
and accept deprivation for the sake of adventure, our passion
for exotic food and music, and especially our shared ecstasy at

nature's beauty turned into a source of easy companionship on the road.

In this state of harmony, I didn't want to remind her that we'd never backpacked before, never slept outdoors—except the night before, surrounded by campers with multiple hookups in a cement tundra off Oregon's Interstate 5—that we had struggled for much longer than the five minutes we were promised it would take to put up the tent, that we had never made a fire, not even in the fireplace at home, because that was father's and brothers' work.

Now, like children playing house, we set to work. Sliding on our backsides to the lake, we bring water back to camp to purify it, a simpler task than I'd imagined. Pitching the tent is more complicated, however. On the soft ground, in full view of both ocean and lake, we unroll the flapping cloth. I am once again lost among the metal poles, struggling to line them up according to the confusing instructions. Seeing my frustration, Daniela takes charge and assigns me the easy task.

"Just open the poles and string them through the loops," she instructs coolly. I can do that, I reason, relieved. As I hold up the interior, she swiftly does whatever it takes outside and turns the floppy nylon into a taut shelter.

I congratulate her profusely, truly impressed, but she shrugs it off.

"It's really simple," she notes, fixing me with those large unblinking eyes, clearly at ease being in charge.

"What's a home without a hearth?" I ask, eager to move beyond the matter of the tent. The fallen wood around us is heavy with dampness. But the beach is gleaming in midday sun, and likely to be littered with dry, light driftwood. We find a narrow path down the steep sand dune.

"It looks like an animal path," she notes, her tone a mixture of inquiry and declaration.

"Maybe," I answer noncommittally.

"What animals do you think use it?" she continues.

"Probably bears," I answer.

She stops and turns around. A ray of fear shines in her confident eyes.

"Maybe only rattlesnakes," I say mischievously, remembering her early and abiding horror of reptiles. Then, my supremacy restored, I add unnecessarily, "Just kidding, just kidding."

The beach stretches on, white, still, devoid of human footprints. It's littered with giant driftwood in fantastic shapes, monstrous redwood trunks carried away, carved by waves and re-deposited on this sandy sculpture park. We walk several miles, examining the horned lions, the winged turtles, the Easter Island heads, running hands over their smooth lines, sitting in their concave interiors. As we dig our feet into the rough sand, the frigid water drains all sensation from our legs, useless columns we haul out to dry in the sun. Nearly dozing on a driftwood lounger, I remember our purpose when my stomach rumbles. Quickly, I call Daniela to order and we begin gathering wood, filling our arms with more than we can carry.

We have long since lost the path back to camp. Searching above the steep face along the ridge, some 400 feet high, yields no clues. My chest tightens.

"It would have been logical to mark the spot," she says. We deposit the driftwood, this time marking the spot with a tall mast, and wander off in opposite directions. Giving up at about the same time, we return to our jumbled pile. I decide we'll bushwhack back to camp. She nods and follows me.

Worn out from counterbalancing the shifting sands, my legs and arms exhausted and aching, I get sloppy and begin dropping the wood. After several stops to rearrange my bundle, she looks at my distraught face, silently picks up the fallen pieces and adds them to her bundle, carrying them without a word. Gratefully, I follow her long, strong legs as we haul ourselves up the last incline and see the tent through the tree trunks.

After a short rest, we boil water on the camp stove and pour it into instant soup, butter bread, prepare tea, and carry everything to the edge of our mountain. Perched like ravens on the cliff's edge, we're at the focal point of the universe. The sun sits on fiery shafts. As we wolf down our dinner, the shafts shorten, dropping the sun into the water. Shadows roll over the ocean like a scroll. We peer across the chasm of darkness, listening closely to the sea of silence.

This is the right time to put a match to the cylindrical bonfire we have prepared. But she reminds me about the food, and about the bears—or maybe just squirrels, I note magnanimously. Yes, I have read that food must be hung, and we have rope and bags to hang from one of the tall trees. But unlike our low-hanging oaks at home, easily climbed, these evergreens are tall and unreachable. How to get the rope high enough off the ground without climbing the tree? We toss the weightless rope up, but it only falls back down at our feet pathetically. I don't recall instructions for this task.

I figure we must tie something heavy to the rope to make it fly. She agrees, and after several failed attempts with pieces of wood, she closes in on a rock.

"How," I ask, "do you intend to tie a rope around a rock and have it stay there while you hurl it?"

Undeterred, her clever fingers fashion a cage of twine around a small rock, which she successfully slings over a branch. Our food bag is hanging some twelve feet up.

"That's too high even for the largest grizzly," she declares with satisfaction.

Now it's finally time. With just a few matches, our little pyramid blossoms, tiny sparks flying from its tongues. The light smoke, sweetened with cones and blackening marshmallows, tickles my nostrils. For at least ten minutes, every pore on my skin opens to the warmth and light.

"We're pretty good, aren't we?" I ask, and she agrees wholeheartedly as we bask in pride and warmth.

The needles and twigs are quickly consumed and the fire becomes an anemic shadow of its blazing self. Our hard-won driftwood refuses to cooperate, barely becoming scorched. We scamper around in the dark, gathering more needles, more twigs, and with each handful the fire flares for a minute or two, then begins to wither.

A stiffening breeze lifts the shirt off my back.

"Do you think it might rain?" she asks.

"Not a chance," I assure her, utterly unsure.

The darkness thickens, amassing a weight that presses onto my bare limbs. The stillness of the afternoon has lapsed into a silence that echoes in my ears. If others are camped anywhere within miles, maybe they don't bother making campfires. Or maybe we're completely alone.

Our fire finally expires in a tiny twist of smoke and a heap of glowing rubies. This is the crucial hour.

"I can't believe no one else is camping in such a perfect place," she says. Her voice is very small in the enormous emptiness around us.

"Are bears attracted to fires or are they afraid of them?" she asks.

"No bears here," I lie with complete confidence. "They never live near oceans."

"But they do in Alaska!" she corrects.

"Those are polar bears, and we're not in a polar region, right?"

No debate here. We establish that no polar bears live within thousands of miles of us. We kill whatever embers remain to mock us, and retreat to the tent.

The sleeping bags retain a bit of the sun's heat and for a little while I feel snug and safe. But the wind—of course it's the wind, right?—whips up a cacophony of unfamiliar noises, fledglings falling out of nests, dry limbs crashing, a tsunami forming, needles and leaves shifting.

"Maybe we should take turns sleeping," she offers.

"O.K., if that makes you feel better. You sleep first and I'll wake you in two hours," I lie again.

I wake in the predawn light to rummaging noises. A bear? Nothing but thin nylon separates us from the 400-pound beast. Is that its haunch I feel brushing the side? Adrenaline surges. The backs of my arms tingle. My throat aches with dryness.

Frozen, I lie very, very still, and the rummaging noises stop. No pounding footsteps leaving either. Maybe it was just a squirrel, making inappropriately loud sounds.

Still, it is impossible to sleep. I lie saucer-eyed as bear stats crowd my brain. There are some half a million black bears in North America. They almost never attack unprovoked, but there are always exceptions.

It's too dark to read, too cold to leave the bag. I lie still and listen for more rummaging noises. Instead, birds begin to pepper the air with song, my signal to move.

The tent zipper wakes Daniela. One eye flies open then promptly shuts.

Outside, the world seems to have grown purer, sharper while I slept. The redwoods, like the spires of medieval cathedrals, are talking to the pale heavens. The ocean's curve reaches farther around, turning our mountain into a tiny spit of land, a tall island in a sea of air. I breathe deeply, exhaling pride, inhaling wonder, exhaling vivid air, inhaling unbounded space. Surely, on the other side of the mountain, a full sun must be rising to make this day as perfect as the last.

But at the moment, the chill is making my nose drip; my numb fingers are aching for a hot cup of coffee to hold. Our food bag is intact, out of reach of bears—and out of my reach, too. Had we ever considered how to get the bag down?

I long desperately for the abominable instant coffee. Peering into the tent, I see that Daniela's sleeping on her back, arms flung up, just as she did in babyhood, and my heart goes slack. I can't wake her in this state of innocence. This means no coffee for hours. Dejected, I go sit by last night's damp embers, pull my hat down farther, shove my hands into pockets, and wait for the sun.

I can't tell if the sky is cloudy or a predawn gray.

Fretting about rain, salivating for bad coffee, I nevertheless doze, and when I wake, the spreading sunrise is reaching up the trunks, nosing into the open tent door.

"Brilliant daughter," I call, knowing her burrowing deeper is a vain attempt. "I've been awaiting your aid all these long hours. Release my coffee, now!"

Once I put on my glasses I can see just how simple it would have been to get at the coffee, but I let her lower the bag, and indulge her tolerant gaze.

The day that unfolds is dazzling, filled with the promise of long, free hours for body and mind to wander. Overcome with the power and glory of having survived the night, we consider staying another. I do raise one feeble objection.

"We don't have enough food," I venture. "We only have the rancid cheese, a can of sardines, bread and peanut butter."

"And tea, and coffee," she adds, as if these were calorie-laden meals. "Oh, and cookies."

"Oh, all four of them," I note dryly.

"We'll be fine. It's already almost lunch, so only a few hours to go before we sleep."

I'm the adult, I tell myself, and not one to ignore hunger. I could argue convincingly, and she'd give in. Then we'd slip back into the careful tolerance, the polite exchanges we both maintain to keep from the adversarial positions her friends and mine have with their mothers and daughters. The idyllic harmony of the past few days, born of our equality in the wild, would vanish. With the coffee still gently warming my insides, it's easy to agree that we may, after all, have enough food for just one more day.

We repeat the foray for wood, now taking our time on the way to the beach to examine the rich vegetation. During the many hours on the train, she read books on the natural history of the Northwest, and now proceeds to regale me with a stream of fascinating facts about red cedar and Douglas fir, Western hemlock and Sitka spruce. As we pass on to the pine- and shrub-covered hills and grassy knolls, I learn about the invasive European beachgrass, and the sensitive Oregon bog anemone, the pink sand verbena and the bugbane. Near the water we spot what looks to me like any plover, but I stand corrected: it's the threatened western snowy plover.

In my garden and the woods behind our house, I taught her what I knew of the local flora and fauna. I now see how the seed I planted has sprouted and ripened into a dazzling flower, far surpassing my own humble knowledge.

Before we hit the beach, we tie a red and a purple bandanna to the shrubs on either side of the path. At lunchtime, they wave us cheerfully back to camp.

But lunch is not enough, and neither is the measly dinner.

I'm not actually hungry, but my stomach feels light, my limbs lack energy. I think of John Muir, who walked for weeks with just bread and tea, satiated by the Sierras' unfolding marvels. I think of Edward Abbey living on beans and muddy Colorado water, nourished by adventure. Then I suggest we finish up the cookies.

"Mom, you know they're our only breakfast, and we'll need energy to pack out, not to sleep," she explains, assuming I don't know the facts as well as she does.

"We'll make it somehow, knowing food is waiting at the car," I counter.

"But that'll be hours after we wake up," she says patiently. "We'll be weak without any starch."

I agree in principle, but can't get those dry cookies off my mind. Seize the moment, I think. I need them now.

We read, write, plan another fire. We watch the sun dip into the ocean, same place, same time, and a show as shockingly beautiful as the last. Afterwards, she leaves for our peeing spot and I see my chance. My mouth is actually watering.

I can't find them. Shocked and embarrassed, I realize she's taken the cookies with her. I retreat to the small fire.

"So what kinds of bears live around here?" she asks nonchalantly.

Now it's my turn to shine. I recite the relevant bear facts I've gleaned from my own reading, carefully staying away from the drama of the rare attacks. Then, I move from earthbound bears to the starlit sky, and together we search for the Milky Way, the North Star, the Big Dipper.

The darkness shrinks our world to the small flame. She moves her rock closer to mine, and I put my arm around her. As she leans gratefully against me, a tremulous sigh escapes her. Every few minutes she swivels her head around, peering into the opaque air, thinking of bears. I tighten my grip on her shoulder and talk about the stars.

Martha Molnar works in public relations and as a freelance writer. She is writing a book about her and her husband's recent move from a New York City suburb to a Vermont hilltop.

KAREN FISHER

* ⁑ *

Mud Night

*When life serves up mud, you might
as well make mud pie.*

THE KIDS WERE SICK OF THE BACK SEAT.

My husband Dave had moved us all to Washington State a few years before, only to become a poster child for Seasonal Affective Disorder. A week before spring break, *he* had broken. We had to leave. Somewhere. Anywhere with sun.

Ellen wanted Paris. She was eleven, a born artist who saw everything as reds and blues and pinks, the painted fingernails of waitresses, the shapes of signs and eyeglasses. She always knew what to wear, and how best to appear normal, even in a family that could not seem to buy Kleenex, or grow a lawn, or get the right smelling detergent.

Grant wanted Hawaii. He was golden, nine years old, and lived for pure velocity, concrete, ramps, and pipes. He was a skater with a dream to surf. In our world of dark forest and gravel, he dreamed of smooth curves, waves, anything bright and fast. Lachlan, who was seven, loved sitting inside with anything small and electronic.

But we were liberally educated, self-employed, downwardly mobile, and somehow always unable to deliver those things our children most desired. Transcendence for us was always somewhere outside, the more remote and difficult to achieve, the better. My mother, having heard the phrase "alternative lifestyle," used it now when explaining us to friends. All were entertained by her stories of us. We lived such interesting lives. On a farm, on a boat, in a tiny island cabin without power. Milling our own logs to lumber. What would we think of next?

Dave said, "Let's drive down to the desert."

"No, Dad," Ellen had said.

"It'll be fun. We'll see wild horses. We'll lie in the sun."

We'd packed our truck with camping gear.

Before children I was always glad to go somewhere to camp with Dave, but now my happiness relied on rare moments when all of us were satisfied. I said, "We'll buy a GameBoy."

The sun came out the day we left. Sky darkened, going south. We drove down through snow and drizzle, hit California in monsoon-like rain. In Indio, drove through dust storms, night lightning. Made camp and watched the clouds roll in. It rained. Black water roared down muddy washes. We read aloud under dripping tarps. We made Indian gambling games from sticks. Woke to frost at Joshua Tree, raced record downpours in Death Valley. In an effort to cheer us all up, I'd at last insisted on getting a hotel in Lone Pine. We'd get a good night's sleep, I said, and get warm in the hot tub. But renovators had left an air compressor in the room underneath us. It roared on and off all night, and the hot tub was ringed in lines of greasy black like a textbook cross-section of the epochs of the earth. It proved Dave's insistence. The best things in life could not be bought, they were all outside somewhere. The very best required four-wheel drive.

But whatever it was—never mind natural beauty, just a little sun, or even *warmth*—we hadn't come close to finding it on this trip, and Dave had been dragging out the miles returning home on narrow mountain roads, still in hope of something that would satisfy. He'd bought a copy of *Hot Springs of the West* that morning when we'd stopped for coffee. Now I was driving, and the audio recording of *Lemony Snickett* had ended, Grant and Lachlan were squabbling to the theme from *Lord of the Rings*, cut with electronic sword-like noises. Grant grabbed for the GameBoy. Lachlan yelled. Ellen thumped Grant and Grant yelled and Ellen yelled and then we both yelled from the front seat for everyone to be quiet.

"Just get along for one more day," I said, "We're on our way home." I was headed for I-5, ready to lay down miles, get a hotel, end up home in time to do the laundry and go shopping for those little snacks that made me feel so good since I had abandoned my objections to individually packaged items, and started putting them in the kids' school lunches.

"Listen to this one," Dave said. "Hunt Hot Springs, near the town of Big Bend. Delightful rock pools on Pitt River near Mount Shasta. Elevation 2,000 feet."

I glanced at the page he showed me, then at him.

I could say no. I should say no. But then vacation would be over, along with Dave's dreams of warmth and wilderness redemption, and it would be my fault.

"O.K.," I said. "But *then* we go straight home."

By nightfall, we'd taken three highways, each smaller and darker and windier than the last. Big Bend was a dead-end town, at the end of a long spur winding down toward the river. Dave was driving. "Read those instructions again," he said.

I read what he'd read to me that morning. Then silently read further. *The dirt road has deteriorated badly making it very rough even for 4WD. Consider hiking in.* I said, "Did you see that warning at the bottom?"

He said, "That's just for low-clearance vehicles."

We had descended, by then, from tall forest through clear-cuts and into scrubby steep-walled valley. Our headlights slid across forlorn trailers, rotting plywood cabins. Barking dogs chained to abandoned cars, the boom-and-bust wasteland with all its human refuse. No natural beauty here. I thought of Lachlan's Game Boy, of evil Sauron's charred and smoking forests. We'd lived in logging country once before, knew the world was not black and white, knew both sides of all good arguments. But I also knew we'd look like owl-loving liberals slipping through enemy lines. This was some tough country.

The guidebook said a single store. We saw it, crossed the bridge. I read by flashlight. "...first fork to the left—"

Dave braked hard, backed up. We rocked in our seats.

"Slow down, *Daaad*," Ellen said, as I read, but he was cranking left as directed, and I *did* see the muddy trough, and the muddy road that followed, but Dave gunned it, careening down hub-deep through pin oak and manzanita, headlights flaring through a herd of cattle. They parted, cows and calves leaping up and into scrubland on both sides as we roared, fishtailed, spinning, spinning, slower and slower down a road as narrow as a flume, nowhere to turn and losing momentum. Trees gave way to a clearing, a sea of pocked and tilted mud. In slow motion we swam through, slower, slower. Mud thundered against wheel wells, rained onto the windshield with even the Game Boy ominously silent. And then we were through, and onto a patch of higher ground.

We got out of the truck, stared into the dark.

Back under the dome light, we looked at the book, and looked into the dark again.

"I think that was the junction," Dave said. "I think we passed it."

"I don't care what we passed," I said. "We're not going down there."

"Let's just look."

We skirted through a patch of oak. A little moon stood above the mist, and by its light we could easily see the right hand road got worse. Also, that a small black truck was stuck there and abandoned. We tried the left hand road. Moonlight shone on puddles as big as ponds, on the melted tracks of skidders. Not even cows had come down here.

Dave said, "Let's turn around."

We got in. Dave started the engine, gunned it backwards at a wild slant, then launched forward, down in a hard right turn through the sea of mud. The truck slewed, slowed, stalled, wheels still spinning. He switched the engine off.

He said, "We're screwed."

"Great," Ellen said. "Why did we even *take* this road?"

I opened the door. The dome light shone on stinking gumbo, deep gray clay and manure. I stepped out. My shoes slipped into deep pocked holes. Fetid geysers squirted up my pant legs and then the yielding clay formed around my feet with an amazing suction. *Splock.* I pulled free, took another step. *Splock. Splock.*

Out the window, Ellen called, "Oh, mom, your shoes!"

Dave said, "I can't believe I did this. Why didn't you stop me from doing this?"

Into the silence that eventually followed, Lachlan said, "Where will we sleep?"

Dave said, "If it rains tonight, we're really *really* screwed."

We opened the tailgate. The dog jumped out. We tossed

chunks of firewood into the slurry for stepping stones, carried the kids to land.

"There's a ring around the moon," Dave said. "It's going to rain."

We got out the tarp. We put the kids in a fireman's line, passed out duffels, tents, foam pads, cold box, guitar, sleeping bags, until we found the mattock and the crate of tools. Dave set to work, in hope of something.

I found a clearing in the woods, got out our tent. The kids, by then, were rising to this occasion.

"No, Grant, you carry this one. Lachlan you carry this," Ellen said. "Mom, do we need all the duffels?"

"No. Let's tarp them. Look at the trees with the moon."

Ellen said, "It's actually really pretty here."

"Is this about as stuck as we've ever been?" Grant asked.

"Yes, *duh*," Ellen said.

I said, "Not many dads are able to get people quite this stuck."

"What time is it?"

"About midnight."

"More like mud-night," Grant said.

We laughed.

"You guys are great," I said. "I'm sorry we were yelling."

"It's O.K.," Ellen said. "Anyway, I wouldn't like it if you guys were just cheesy. I definitely wouldn't like a cheesy mom."

"What's a cheesy mom?"

"All fake and boring."

Lachlan asked, "Will it rain tonight?"

I said, "It might."

"If it rains, what will happen to the truck?"

"It'll get more stuck," I said. "We might not get out for a long time."

"*How* long?" Ellen asked.

"If it really rains, it could be many days."

"Cool," said Grant.

Clearly being stuck in the mud was not worse than being stuck in school.

"Then the truck will sink?" Lachlan asked.

"Yes it will," I said, snapping the poles together, squinting in the moonlight to see which were black and which were gold.

Stricken, he said, "But the *Game Boy* is inside."

I saw his vision, pouring rain and the mud slowly rising, sealing doors, covering windows, oozing over the roof in cartoon bubbles. I laughed. "Not that deep," I said. "The Game Boy's safe."

Dave came back through the trees. The tent was up. Our things lay tarped against the coming rain.

"Well?"

"Even if I could jack it up and get under it, I'd only gain a couple of feet." How long would it take to cross a sea of mud two feet at a time? He said, "We might as well enjoy those hot springs."

We found flashlights, towels, and followed the dog down the slippery road. Forty yards away the small black truck, now companion to our own, was also a warning: smashed glass, garbage, moldy seats. The road got steeper. Grant's flashlight beam swept over a desolate tan sedan with four flat tires, seats gone, trunks sprung.

Our big red truck was the first good thing that Dave and I had earned together—it was work and play, firewood, construction, hauling hay; it was dump runs, ski trips, camping. It was literally a part of us. Now each bend toward the river brought another metal corpse, someone's joyride, some dad's borrowed car, some nice young couple up from U.C. Davis for whom that day had ended with someone yelling, "Why didn't you stop me?" All those cars. All those fatal desires.

"In any reasonable place, there'd have been a sign," I said. Even with the moon and oaks I'd sensed the sinister possibility that the people of Big Bend had divined our various weaknesses, were waiting, wondering what the night had trapped.

We found the pools, described accurately, very pleasant. I sat imagining the coming day and who we'd find and how they'd read our muddy clothes, our straight white teeth, our uncut hair. Dave's boots had fallen out the back of the truck when we'd lost the tailgate in Death Valley, and all he had were Tevas. We had forty dollars, and the Visa wouldn't save us.

In our tent, we lay awake.

Dave kept sighing. The dog growled, then quieted. Rain came and passed. The children breathed. I'd almost gone to sleep when Dave said, "I can trade the gun."

"What *gun?*"

He'd brought his pistol, he explained. That cheap Saturday Night Special he'd bought that first year we'd sold Christmas trees. He'd thrown it in at the last minute.

In the morning, we left the dog and kids with bacon, walked the road a mile to find the store. A man who looked like Willie Nelson was opening it. He said his name was Freddy. Freaky Freddy.

"Hot springs," he said. We were both head-to-toe in mud. We admitted it.

"Four-wheel drive?"

We admitted that, too.

"That's your first mistake." He said, "Bill's got a skidder, but he won't go down there now."

We talked. Shrugged, sighed. Identical men, each three hundred pounds and missing teeth, shuffled forward to buy a case of Pepsi. We nodded, watched, talked a little more. With inspired staging, I told Dave I should get back to the kids, they'd be wondering where we were.

"You got *kids* up there?"

"Yeah," I smiled and shrugged. "They're O.K., though. They're pretty tough campers. I think we'll be all right till spring."

Dave said, "You know, I do have a gun I could trade someone for help getting out."

"Well," Freddy said, "let's see who else we know."

Gaylord and Jim were both on disability and showed up from across the road to see the gun. By midday we had ropes and strapping, logs and chains and strips of cyclone fencing, trucks and ATVs. We were all good friends and I'd decided I probably wouldn't be all that unhappy if we just ended up in Big Bend.

Almost too soon we were out. Gaylord invited us to look at all his guns. By the time we'd finished borrowing his hose, the only deep thing left was gratitude.

Back on the highway we pulled off at Shasta rest area, the Dodge still shedding lumps of clay, our clothes and shoes now stiff and ludicrously heavy. We opened the camper and looked in: tools, tent, duffel. It was hard to tell what color any of it might have been. The muddy dog jumped down. We got out a muddy picnic for our muddy kids, clomped over to a spigot by the sidewalk. Clean water poured into a tidy metal drain. We scrubbed, watching clean people get out of clean cars to walk their clean leashed dogs, escort clean children to the restroom. They all looked carefully away, so as not to encourage us. Maybe this was the real divide—nothing to do with politics or money or education, with what you cut down in your life or left standing, but everything to do with who stayed on the wide roads, and who ventured off them.

I grinned and called the dog.

"Those were good hot springs," Dave said. "We should go again sometime."

Grant agreed. He said, "It was kind of fun getting stuck."

"I can't believe his name was actually Gaylord," Ellen said, who had been almost fatally teased that year by a girl who liked, inexplicably, to call her by that name. And now Gaylord was our hero. He'd said maybe after all that rain, they ought to put up a sign.

But what sign would have convinced us, when no amount of money buys transcendence, and you can't get there without four-wheel drive?

Karen Fisher's debut novel, A Sudden Country, *earned numerous awards, including the Sherwood Anderson Foundation Award and the VCU First Fiction award, and was a finalist for many others, including the* L.A. Times *Art Seidenbaum and PEN/Faulkner Awards for fiction. She lives with her family on an island off the coast of Washington.*

* * *

The Bears Will Eat You

*Pregnancy felt like a natural disaster until her
own mother-bear instinct kicked in.*

I CONCENTRATED ON THE *TICK TICK TICK* SOUND OF THE
hot engine cooling and tried not to throw up. Heat rose in
fuzzy waves from the hood of the car. In two days we put over
a thousand miles on her.

I was well into my seventh miserable month of pregnancy
when we pulled up to the rented log cabin that represented
our last vacation as a childless couple. Glacier National Park
was just a few miles away. A million acres of pristine nature
and jagged peaks, Glacier sits on the northern border of
Montana. Emerald mountain ridges, rivers of gentle turquoise
and places named Garden Wall and Goat Haunt make up this
paradise on earth.

Jesse was fully accustomed to the "pregnancy car routine"—get out of the car, run to the passenger side, open door,
extend hands to support weight of bulging wife. Escort
bulging wife to room. Make several trips back and forth from
the room to the car to retrieve luggage and supplies. I knew
that traveling with me so pregnant was hard on Jesse, but it's
harder for a woman the morning she wakes up and weighs
more than her husband.

The ultrasound told us to expect a boy. The freckled, expressionless nurse stared at black-and-white blobs on the screen as she pressed a cold, goopy device onto my full belly. I squeezed my bladder with military force to prevent an accident. Nurse tapped on her keyboard several times, saving screenshots of unidentifiable objects. Suddenly she announced "It's a penis!" and pointed at what I thought might have been a foot, or an ear. Jesse whooped loudly. Finally there would be someone to watch college basketball with.

I was crushed. I was certain there was a girl in there. I had spent my increasing bouts of insomnia fantasizing about taking my daughter hiking and showing her how to change a tire. She would be strong, shun pink, and climb mountains, having received all of my ruggedized X chromosomes.

"Sometimes ultrasounds are wrong, right?" I asked the nurse hopefully.

"Sometimes," she said, nodding. "But not the ones that clearly show a penis."

I held back tears. Lately, I was hormonal over puppy food commercials, but this news really hurt. I tried not to feel betrayed by Jesse's elation. What was I going to do with a boy? *For that matter, what are you going to do with a baby?* I had already promised Jesse that I would never call the baby an "accident." In his family, *miracle* was the accepted moniker for an unplanned pregnancy. I had to remind myself of this every day since the miraculous pink line had appeared in the second window.

After showers and catnaps, we drove back to Kalispell and found a steakhouse. Jesse ordered a twelve-ounce tenderloin and the tallest beer on the menu. I was hungry, but my stomach was competing for space with the rest of my internal organs. I ordered a simple side of mashed potatoes.

"What!" Jesse scoffed at my order. "You have to order a steak! It's a steakhouse."

"I'm not that hungry," I lied.

Jesse's face fell. He wanted to celebrate our vacation. *If I could drink a damn beer, I would want to celebrate too,* I thought. I gave in and ordered a New York strip well done, though I am a medium-rare kind of gal. Alas, all pregnancy books forbid the consumption of meat that has not been cooked to leather.

The waitress didn't write our order down, but I heard her reciting it to the cooks perfectly. I am always impressed when a waitress remembers an entire order without writing it down. I stared at cattle ranch-themed décor bolted to the walls of the restaurant. Saddles. Horseshoes. The depressing, glass-eyed head of a bull.

I was not a happy pregnant woman. The glow must have skipped me and gone to the next lady in line. What I couldn't admit to Jesse was this: I resented pregnancy. The heartburn, the constant peeing, the aching joints, the lack of sleep…I resented every last part of the "miracle." I felt fat. Beefy. I could be mounted on the wall of the restaurant, and no one would think it odd. Worst of all, I feared that I would surely resent the baby inside of me.

Jesse unfolded a map of the park. "What should we do tomorrow?"

"Going to the Sun?" I suggested. I could sense the wheels turning in his mind. Jesse is a photographer. He was considering tomorrow's weather forecast, sunrise and sunset, and where the moon would be in the sky. He was considering the wind.

"It's supposed to be breezy and overcast tomorrow," he said. "Let's go to Polebridge instead. We can do Going to the Sun on Tuesday." Jesse continued to study the map until the waitress arrived with our food. I passed the time trying to imagine myself joining the PTA. Thankfully the food arrived quickly.

I cut into my steak to find it cool, red, and bleeding in the center. Not just medium rare, but woefully, wonderfully undercooked. I lusted after the rawness of this forbidden meat. My tongue tingled with desire. But there was the baby. A fetus, really, but a fetus I was responsible for. A fetus that was preventing me from consuming the luscious steak sitting in front of me that I had ordered out of guilt. I refused to bother the waitress. She wasn't pregnant. She wasn't responsible for the growing of a human being. She just wouldn't understand.

I burst into tears.

People stared. I cried into my steak. I wailed, shouldering the burden of all pregnant women throughout history. The waitress darted to our table and offered help, which made me wail louder.

Jesse was mortified. The dead bull on the wall witnessed it all with its sad glass eyes. At that moment, my intense hatred of pregnancy eclipsed all other hatreds in the world, even my hatred of cheerleaders.

The waitress rushed the steak back to the kitchen. Jesse uttered niceties, trying to make me feel better. The steak was returned to me a warm beige color. It tasted like sorrow. The waitress kindly packed the leftovers into a foam box. I dropped the box into the trash on the way out the door. *Plop*.

That night I tossed and turned and searched for a sleeping position that didn't cut off the feeling in my legs. I prayed that I wouldn't hate my baby when he came into the world. I was a failure at motherhood before I was a mother, having to pray for what I was supposed to feel naturally. The books don't prepare you for this.

We drove to Polebridge the next morning.

Polebridge is a blink of a town in northern Glacier, at the end of a long gravel road. We drove up to the general store in search of a soda and a small meal to take with us to the lake. A picnic might make up for the previous evening. A one-eyed cat stood guard on the porch of the store. Marigolds erupted from of a pair of dirt-filled boots. Weathered rocking chairs with missing back rails beckoned visitors to sit a spell. Inside the store, the floor had a perceptible tilt. Bare earth was visible through cracks. I waddled carefully to the cooler and picked out an orange soda. Jesse bought two pork sandwiches while I claimed the empty rockers on the porch. We ate. In the distance, the Canadian Rockies stood watch. We basked in the scenery and listened to the locals converse and drink their black coffee.

"Grizzlies?" one man asked another.

"Two," the other replied. "Seen 'em in the clearing near the bridge. Went back with Pete fifteen minutes later and they was gone."

"You sure it wasn't a brown?"

"Course I'm sure."

The men continued to talk and laugh and the subject was changed.

"Maybe we'll see a bear," Jesse said.

"I hope not," I said.

A voice from the past invaded my mind. It was my mother's voice, transporting me back to my youth. She was interrogating me, the same way she did each time I did something outdoorsy. Growing up in Montana, outdoorsy is hard to avoid.

"You're not on your period, are you?"

"Mom! God."

"Grizzly bears can smell women on their period!" She glared at me and shook her head.

"Mom, you always worry about dumb things," I said.

"It's not dumb," she insisted. "You better not go on any hikes if you're on your period!"

"Mom! Leave me alone!"

"They can smell it from miles and miles away!"

"Mom, stop! I'm Not! On! My! Period!"

"The bears will eat you!"

"Here's the lake," Jesse said, bringing me back to the present. He pointed to a blue blob on the map. I noticed how far north we were. The lake was several miles north of Polebridge.

"Let's go," I said, resisting the urge to protest. The chances that I would go into labor early in the middle of Glacier National Park were slim, but I didn't want to take chances when I was so unbalanced. Pioneers may have been capable of birthing a child in the middle of the woods, but I did not want to recreate any scenes from the *Little House* books. Had Laura given birth? Mary? Ma? How did they boil water?

The road to the lake was annoyingly rugged. Too much orange soda at the general store. Jesse stopped the car three times for me, and thanks to my looming belly obscuring the view, I peed on my shoes twice.

Jesse navigated through a shallow stream and over a tricky series of rocks, and we finally arrived at the Bowman Lake campground. We parked next to two bear-proofed garbage cans. A sign indicated that the lake was a short hike away, just down a woodsy trail.

"This place is gorgeous," Jesse said. I nodded. The sky was perfect—fluffy cotton clouds drifting against an impossible blue. I inhaled deeply, memorizing the scent of the air. We headed down the trail. Technicolor wildflowers lined the path. Loons echoed in the distance. It was a magical place.

A quiet thought slipped into my mind. I want to take my son here, where the silence was its own life force. He—my child—would need to know that there were still wild places in the world.

Soon I was panting my way down the trail. My growing son was doing a number on my lung capacity.

"Are you feeling O.K.?" Jesse asked.

"I'm—what was that?" I perked up. A sharp crack came from deep in the bushes.

"It sounds like someone's chopping wood," Jesse said. But the only car in the parking area had been ours.

Crack!

"Hello?" Jesse called out loud enough so that anyone in the woods would hear. No answer.

Crack, crack!

"I'm going to go up the trail and see," Jesse said.

"What if it's a bear?" I said.

"It's not a bear," Jesse said. He disappeared around a corner.

I stayed frozen on the trail and listened. Only moments ago I was certain that this was a silent place. Silent it was not. The buzz of a million insects pollinating and procreating filled the air with electricity. The ground teemed with marching ants. The beat of wings from above left a vibration in the air. My own breathing seemed ridiculously loud. *People have no business here,* I thought. Especially pregnant people.

How long had Jesse been gone? What if it *was* a bear? What if the bear was watching me right now? Could bears smell pregnancy like they smelled periods? Were human fetuses the veal of the bear world?

The bears will eat you.

I couldn't stand it anymore. I slowly tiptoed into the bushes. I didn't have to go far, as Jesse appeared from the trail. His face was ashen; a finger held to his lips. *Shhh.* He pointed through an opening in the pines.

An enormous, coffee-colored bear was tearing into a log. The bear's unmistakable hump—the incredibly powerful muscle that allowed its forearms to shred logs and skulls—indicated that it was a grizzly. My blood ran cold.

The bears will eat you.

Surprising a bear is insanely dangerous. When bears hear human-made noises, they usually disappear long before they are ever discovered. This bear hadn't heard us…or perhaps he just wasn't afraid. I pivoted on the trail, trying to stay quiet. Pregnant women don't flee gracefully. Pregnant women *lumber.* I lumbered down the trail with Jesse behind me.

Crack! Crack!

The adrenaline kicked in. I talked to my son in my mind. *Baby, I won't let us get eaten.* I imagined the bear behind us on the trail, and the hair on my neck stood up. *Sweet, sweet child. I won't let you down.* My heart raced. I moved faster. *Good, good baby, don't worry, Mommy loves you so much.* I now felt that I could sprint all the way home, away from grizzlies, away from danger. *I'm sorry baby! I am sorry I had so many bad thoughts about you. I don't resent you.* It was too far to run to the car. Jesse grabbed my hand and we scrambled down a side trail to the lake.

I followed the lakeshore as long as I could. I was tired and breathing hard. My hands shook. The baby was kicking and twisting. Somersaults of joy? "I love you," I said with a voice only he could hear. Tears welled in my eyes.

"We're O.K.," Jesse said. "I think we're pretty far now."

The tears spilled over. I couldn't explain the sudden joy and love that flooded my heart. *I love you, and I will always protect you.*

My eyes scanned the curve of the lake. A few hundred yards in the distance, a great golden bear emerged from the trees. A tiny bear followed, joining its mother on the shore. The mother grizzly bristled. Piercing, wild eyes met mine. I held my breath and placed a hand on my belly. *It's O.K.*, I whispered in my mind. *I'm a mother too.*

The grizzly turned her powerful body to the forest and galloped into the trees with her baby ambling safely behind her.

Maleesha Speer is a software engineer, writer, and blogger. She lives in Gallatin County, Montana—a place teeming with grizzly bears.

*   *   *

From the Mouths of Babes

Move swiftly, don't whine, and try your hardest.

THE LAST TIME I SAW COACH HIS BODY WAS PUFFY. His chiseled face was unchanged—flat lips, deep eyes, dark hair, still as handsome as the young Clint Eastwood—but he looked as if he were wearing someone else's inflated, definitionless body.

The disease had progressed that far. I was at the top of a climb with several friends when he appeared at the base of the smooth granite wall. It struck me as strange to see him just standing there on the ground rather than climbing.

All of us up on the ledge had once been his athletes. Coach had led us and the rest of the Laramie High School swim team to seven consecutive state championship titles. He was a man at once compassionate, taciturn, and merciless. Every day for years Coach got us to swim till our bodies turned to lead—till our legs couldn't move and our arms couldn't come out of the water. He made the strongest swim 400, 500, 600 laps. Some of these laps were fifty-yard sprints against the clock. They were almost unbearable, and yet we did it. Coach constantly, if often wordlessly, pushed us to go faster, try harder. We never complained, but everybody thought this was outrageous, because everybody thought we were only training for the state meet—except Coach. He knew the meet would come and go and then we'd graduate and the trophies would disappear into boxes and what he'd helped make of us would be all that was left.

Besides commanding the swim team, he'd taught P.E. classes in swimming, karate (he was a black belt, naturally), and rock climbing. Karate demanded too much quiet discipline for most of us hormone-fueled jocks, and more swimming was out of the question, so we signed up for rock climbing. Every morning until the mountains were buried in snow, Coach drove a school bus up to the rocks in the dark so we would be climbing by dawn and back to school by second period. In the biting mornings of late fall and early spring our fingers would become so numb we could hardly feel the rock.

That was a decade and a half earlier. Now Coach was staring up at us, squinting into the sun. It was a gorgeous Wyoming autumn afternoon: not a cloud, not a breath of wind, air crisp as kindling. We shouted down, asking him if he'd brought his rock shoes along. He shook his head but then motioned for us to lower the rope. We glanced at each other. We were at the top of Fall Wall, an infamous 5.10 route composed of nothing but tiny eighth-inch holds, the kind that require precise edging with tight rock shoes. Coach was in running shoes, with no harness.

When the rope reached him he picked up the end, tied it around his waist with a bowline, looked up and yelled, "On belay?"

In the beginning, Coach had taught us how to climb without a harness as well—how to just wrap the rope around your waist several times, tie a knot called the bowline-on-a-coil, and go. It was the mid-'70s. In Wyoming, the ethics of climbing were still largely descended from mountaineering, as were the techniques and the gear. We climbed on ropes stiff as lariats using aluminum nuts and iron pitons for protection. Knowing your knots mattered. Route-finding mattered. A climber of conscience climbed only what he could lead in good style. No hangs, no falls, no excuses. I never saw Coach climb any other way. It was a matter of pride, of character. Today people climb harder, but not bolder.

"Belay on!" I answered.

And Coach started to climb.

The moment he touched the rock his bloated, betrayed body was transformed. It was as though he had stepped into a world without gravity. He climbed with utter silence and grace. Each movement was discrete and intentional and yet he seemed to flow up the wall, like water in reverse. Every foot placement was sure and confident and his feet stuck to the rock like glue. It didn't matter that his sloppy shoes couldn't possibly use the tiny edges. *If you believe your feet will stick, they'll stick.* That's what Coach used to tell us when we were halfway up a climb and our feet started slipping and we started whining.

I made my first lead with Coach. I'd only done three or four climbs when he handed me two pieces of gear and pointed up to a 5.7 off-width called Upper Slot. I put in both pieces of protection low on the climb, got about twenty feet above the second piece, and froze. Too scared to go up, incapable of climbing down, I hung there like a frightened kitten. Coach watched and waited. After a while I started to tremble, then shake. Soon fear had taken over so completely I was shuddering. Coach yelled at me to get my head together and just finish the climb, but by now I had already lost my head. I was puling shamelessly and fatigue was sickening me and I was losing my grip and my feet were slipping off. I was certain I was going to fall and die ignominiously when Coach soloed up behind me. Standing steady as a solid platform right under my feet, he handed up a fist-sized piece of protection, a #11 hexentric, and told me in a calm, stern voice to put it in and climb to the top, which I did.

Twenty-five years of climbing and I have never been as scared since. For a long time I thought he had been cruel, because I thought Coach was merely trying to teach me how to rock climb, how to be a rock climber. But most of Coach's students never became rock climbers. I'm sure he didn't expect they would. They would forget the skill but perhaps remember the will.

That autumn afternoon, Coach climbed Fall Wall as fluidly as a dancer. He did it in worn-out running shoes with a body that was no longer his. Unlike every other coach I ever had, and for that matter almost any person I've met, Coach was a man who expected more from himself than from you. When he got to the top he didn't say a word. He momentarily flashed his Man-With-No-Name smile. I never saw him again.

Coach Layne Kopishka died of hemochromatosis—a disease in which there is too much iron in the blood—on July 11, 1992, just a few months after my first daughter was born. He left behind a wife, Judy, and two daughters, Shawna and Tonya. Coach was forty-seven.

Not long ago I started trying to teach my daughters how to rock climb. At the time, Addi was six and Teal was three.

We didn't go to the climbing gym. My girls like playing on the artificial wall, but when you're in a box with a roof rather than outside beneath the sky, surrounded by walls instead of horizons and fluorescent light instead of sunshine, you learn very different things. We went into the mountains, to a dome of rounded pink granite named the Rat Brain, not far from Upper Slot and Fall Wall.

There were six of us in all, if you count Meggie, our chocolate Lab: Addi and Teal, their six-year-old friend Justin, me, and my friend Ed, a philosophy professor who has more patience and compassion than I do, which is why I recruit him for instructional adventures.

Stepping out of the truck we were blasted by a cold wind and everyone donned wool caps and windbreakers. We had backpacks, water bottles, apples, climbing harnesses, locking carabiners, and belay devices. Addi brought along her books, Justin brought his ratty down jacket, Teal brought her stuffed seal.

The path along the top of the beaver dam where we usually crossed the creek was flooded, so we had to search for another route across. The kids ran upstream and discovered a game trail through a meadow that leaped the creek and wove on through the willows. Above the creek we discovered a lean-to hidden in the aspens: fallen logs angled against a boulder blackened from a fire pit. Addi, Justin, and Teal wanted to stay and play, but I insisted they keep moving.

(Just a note: One of the many ridiculous maxims that have been whirling about in Dadland since the late 1960s is: *Never push or pull your child. Let your child do exactly what she wants and she'll naturally rise to her potential.* Spare me. We all push and pull our kids; the questions are how, when, and to what degree.)

On the lower slabs of rock beyond the trees, I had to hand the kids up to Ed at several difficult places, but Meggie, a rock dog who's been going into the mountains with me since she was three months old, used her clawed paws like a double set of crampons, forcefully scratching her way up. A climbing buddy of mine swears he's seen Meggie do a pull-up.

This was our second outing. We'd all come to the Rat Brain a week before and it had turned into a battlefield where Ed and I suffered an ignoble defeat: the kids had started whimpering, saying they didn't like rock climbing and refusing to continue.

Teal had bounced back the very next day, asking when we would get to go back. (Being three, I think she was enthralled by the name Rat Brain.) A few days later Justin left a message on my office phone machine asking to go climbing again. But Addi, an intellectual at six, would not let the rosy light of nostalgia color her harsh experience. The only way I got her to go a second time was by promising her that she didn't have to climb unless she wanted to. Hence the books stuffed in her pack alongside her harness. She could read while Justin and Teal climbed.

When we arrived at the base of the Rat Brain it was so windy the kids were getting knocked over. Teal, Justin, and Addi hid behind a boulder with their noses running. Even Ed admitted it was cold. But soon enough they got themselves occupied. Justin checked out the "bathtub"—an erosion hollow in the rock filled with snowmelt—for insects. I could see none but he of course found loads. Justin is a born naturalist. Addi sat down, got out her books and began to read, grasping the pages tightly so they wouldn't flap. Teal started playing with the carabiners, linking them together like paper clips. None of them was the least bit interested in climbing.

Nonetheless, Ed scaled the cerebrum of the Rat Brain and clipped in the ropes while I got each of the kids into their harnesses. They ignored me, moving their arms and legs automatically while continuing to play or read. I asked Justin if he wanted to go first; he said he'd rather continue plucking bugs out of the mud. I reminded him that he had called me to go climbing.

"Ohhh-kaayy." He stood up, heaved his narrow shoulders, and jiggled the rope indifferently.

I belayed while Ed soloed beside Justin, giving moral support, pointing out handholds and footholds, and demonstrating the proper body position for face climbing. Justin's gym shoes were too big and they peeled off halfway up. He had to be lowered in his socks and Ed secured the shoes on his feet by wrapping them with athletic tape. After that he climbed well, if slowly, pretending to be scared but concentrating. At the top he threw his arms into the cold blue sky and let out a whoop.

Teal was next. Ed belayed, I climbed alongside. She never looked back, or down for that matter. She was soon to turn four—as she told everyone—and considered herself the equal of any six-year-old. Ignoring my advice on where to put her feet and which handholds to hang onto, simply assuming her little feet inside her little tennis shoes would stay wherever she placed them, she scampered straight to the top. I showed her how to throw her hands in the air like Justin, and she did it, but she didn't get it. Climbing up a cold rock face in wind that could lift her off her feet just wasn't that big a deal. On the other hand, she throws her hands in the air all the time when we put on music in the living room. She loves to dance.

There are purportedly dads who still believe teaching is a one-way street. You preach, they pray. In fact, you learn immediately that teaching is a wide, two-way boulevard with lots of crazy traffic, ideas, and education zooming both directions. If you're teaching a kid, then the kid is teaching you back.

Addi knew I had promised her I wouldn't force her, but she also knew I wouldn't leave her alone. She gave in after repeated coaxing. Ed belayed and I coached. Up on the rock her genuine fear of heights reasserted itself. She was only five feet off the ground when her legs began to tremble. She tried to move up and her feet slipped and her fingernails dug desperately into the rock. She was on the verge of tears. I felt like a shit.

"Addi, calm down." I had my hand on her back. "Look for something to put your feet on." I pointed out two small dishes in the rock.

She listened. She focused. She placed the toes of her hiking boots on the slopey concavities and her body relaxed slightly.

"All right! See that?"

She gave me a grim smile. She kept climbing, but she didn't go all the way to the top. At the start she had told me that she would climb to the second bolt and no farther. I'd told her that when she got that high she would want to keep going. She didn't. She wanted to come down. Still, when she got back on the ground she was beaming.

Justin agreed to tie in again only if I promised to watch over the cup of bugs he had collected. He was planning to bring them home to show his mom. I obviously didn't understand the value of insects, so he didn't trust me: while he was climbing he kept looking down to make sure his bugs were safe.

When I asked Teal if she wanted to climb again she lightheartedly said no. Then seconds later, just as gaily, she said yes. She roped in and flitted up the wall and came down and went back to reorganizing my spare carabiners.

Addi, inspired by her first success, climbed to the second bolt again, but even with urging wouldn't go higher. She came down and went back to reading.

While Ed and I coiled the ropes, the kids ate their apples and drank from their water bottles and wiped their noses and stared out across the frigid mountains. The truck was a mile away and we raced back, Ed and I getting them all to run to stay warm. They each took several rough tumbles in the woods before we reached the truck. We piled in, I cranked up the heat, and we began grinding homeward along the jeep road.

Once we were back on the highway, after everyone was warm and before the knock-knock jokes started, I asked our three small climbers if they could tell me one thing that they'd learned. It could only be one thing, the most important thing.

They sat quietly for a moment, thinking. I expected them to say something technical about rock climbing—"Don't hug the rock" or "Don't use your knees" or "Look for footholds"—one of the rules Ed and I had exposited.

Justin was resting his head on Ed's shoulder. He looked subdued, a rare state for a boy like Justin, but then he screwed up his face, his cheeks suddenly red as cherries, and shouted, "Move swiftly!"

I looked at Teal. She already had her answer. She threw her hands in the air and yelled, "Don't whine!"

Addi, glowing with pride, quietly said, "Try your hardest."

Ed slapped his thighs.

The next day Ed, the philosopher, told me he had gone home, written their lessons down, and taped them on his wall.

Move swiftly. Don't whine. Try your hardest.

If Coach were still alive I would have written him a letter and told him this story. But then he already knew it. So I'm writing you.

Mark Jenkins also contributed "The Snowcave" to this collection.

✱ ✱ ✱

Surviving Scout Camp

Even if you can't take the city out of the mom,
you can take the mom out of the city.

THANKS TO MY PREVIOUS CAREER AS A TRAVEL EDITOR, I
know how to rate a mattress and a motel bathroom. I'm right
at home in a wicker rocker on the porch of a quiet country
inn, sipping a tall glass of iced tea while watching the sun dip
behind a mountain range.

But until my son joined Cub Scouts, my getaways did not
include wilderness adventures. To me, communing with nature
meant reading Thoreau, potting begonias, or maybe collecting
shells near a beachfront vacation condo. Spending a weekend in
the woods of rural Michigan—with a chorus of bullfrogs,
sundry snakes, ticks, two dozen little boys, and their suburban-
Detroit mothers—didn't sound like my idea of a good time.

Like most parents, however, I've learned to adapt. And
while I am not exactly what you'd call a happy camper, the
Scouts have taught me to appreciate the Great Outdoors. In
fact, this fall I'll embark on my third annual "Mom & Me"
camping weekend with Nate's pack.

These weekends, I've discovered, were devised to encourage mother-and-son bonding, and to refute the theory that
women will not sleep with insects. I've also learned that the

travel writer's motto, "Always pack light," doesn't apply to north woods camping. On our first outing, for instance, Nate fell into a bog within fifteen minutes of our arrival at the campsite. He had to borrow my hiking boots until his own dried out the next day. Meanwhile, I had no choice but to tour the swamp in soggy tennis shoes.

"This weekend is an endurance test for parents," one mom confided, half-seriously.

The following year I stuffed half a dozen pairs of boots into the back of our Jeep, but forgot my own raincoat. Of course, that was the weekend it poured and poured…and poured.

I'll never forget the sight of six devoted moms building a campfire in the evening drizzle. (We were determined to do this thing right: we were going to roast every single hot dog and melt every marshmallow we'd hauled along with our Duraflame logs.) Our boys, however, were smart enough to hide from the rain. Desperately searching the campground by flashlight, we finally found them hunkered down in one of the cabins playing Life, the board game of the moment.

"Bring the hot dogs in here, ladies," one nine-year-old de-manded as he scooted his car-shaped marker across the board. "I'm getting ready to sell one of my houses and I'm having a midlife crisis!"

If we're very lucky, the hike to the public restrooms is only fifteen minutes (uphill) from our campsite. The trick, I found, is to keep a spare flashlight in your sleeping bag so that you can grab it quickly if nature calls at 2 A.M.

Nobody sleeps much on these weekends. The kids are buzzing on caffeine, having consumed several gallons of Pepsi and Mountain Dew. The moms, smelling like a bonfire and desperately wishing for one hot shower, toss fitfully in their sleeping bags while the boys play flashlight games and tell ghost stories.

"Did you hear the one about the one-eyed man who went berserk in the north woods and was *never found...*?"

After two nights like these, the long drive back home on Sunday is tolerable only with a mug of instant coffee and the promise of a warm bath. Completely exhausted, Nate and I usually ride home in silence, barely acknowledging the panoramic blur of farms, fields, and factories beyond the windows of our Jeep.

But last October, on the way home, he mumbled, "Thanks for the weekend, Mom.... Great weekend." It was a rare moment of sincere, unprompted gratitude.

Catching a glimpse of myself in the rearview mirror, I remembered I wasn't wearing makeup. My eyes looked older, and in an instant I saw the years racing past me like the cars on the expressway. My boy looked older, too, his lanky body slouched on the seat next to me.

Suddenly, that weekend—my endurance test—seemed awfully short. I was proud of myself for hiking swamps and building fires in the rain, but most of all, I was thankful that I had shared these experiences with my son.

Cindy La Ferle is a widely published newspaper columnist, essayist, and writing teacher based in Royal Oak, Michigan. Her essays and features have appeared in many national magazines and anthologies, including Reader's Digest, The Christian Science Monitor, Writer's Digest, Guideposts, The Detroit News and Free Press, *and many others. She is author of* Writing Home, *her own award-winning essay collection focusing on home and family issues. She's currently at work on a midlife memoir about restoring and living in a Frank Lloyd Wright home. Visit her website at* www.laferle.com.

JOHN N. FELSHER

✳ ✳ ✳

Hunting with Daniel

*One man's rugged test of endurance comes
in the form of his five-year-old son.*

IT LOOKED LIKE A GOOD DAY FOR HUNTING—COOL, CALM,
and quiet. A crisp autumn chill had turned the leaves various
shades of orange, scarlet, and gold.

I crept through the forest, pausing frequently to scan for
my elusive quarry. Carefully, I eased my foot softly, gently to
the ground, taking great care not to crack a twig. Then all of
a sudden, I heard it.

"*Boom, pow!* Get the bad guys. I'm a cowboy hunting buf-
faloes. *Bang, bang!*"

"Daniel, you have to be quiet in the woods. You'll scare the
game," I instructed my then five-year-old son.

"O.K., Daddy, I'll be quiet. You won't hear nothin' out of
me. Why are we being quiet? When are we going to see animals? Have I been quiet long enough yet? If I'm quiet can I
shoot the gun? Huh, Daddy, can I, can I? I'll shoot it real quietly. Watch how far I can throw this pinecone. Watch, Daddy.
You won't hear another word out of me, Daddy, I'll be—"

"*Hush!*"

The sport of hunting offers many supreme challenges.
Sportsmen have downed elephants with longbows and primitive

arrows, entered grizzly bear dens armed with only a knife, and faced charging rhinos with stone-tipped spears. However, those feats pale against hunting anything with a small child.

Hunting with children takes the patience of Job and the wisdom of…O.K., actually not much wisdom. Did I mention the patience of Job?

To start off, children, especially little boys, are naturally curious and have attention spans measured in seconds. They pocket any pretty leaf, misshapen acorn, shiny rock, or other treasure. They grab bugs, preferring dangerous ones like spiders and wasps. And, above all, they cannot keep still and quiet.

"Daniel, let's sit here and listen for animals."

"O.K., Daddy. Is this a good spot? Where are the animals going to come from? When are we going to see something? I'm hungry. Can I have my snacks now?"

"Hush," I repeated, extending a shaky hand for the coffee jug so I could get another jolt of caffeine.

"Daddy, let me do it. I'll pour it. Oops!"

"*Yeowwwww!*"

"Gee, Daddy, that jug we gave you for Father's Day sure keeps coffee hot. Sorry, Daddy. I kind of dumped the rest on the ground when you hollered. I'll scoop it up for you."

"Never mind. I'm on a special low-dirt diet."

Finally, after threatening to cut off his snack supply, I persuaded Daniel to keep his mouth shut for a few moments. After about fifteen seconds of blissful peace, I heard a strange tearing sound and then thought I heard the sound of an animal scurrying through the weeds. I was wrong.

Daniel, while keeping his mouth shut, was tearing off sections of a rotting log and rolling the big pieces down a small hill.

"Daniel, aren't you supposed to be keeping quiet?"

"I'm not saying nothing, Daddy. It's just my hands making noise. I shut up."

Being out in the woods with a child allows an experienced parent to share knowledge of the forest denizens.

"Daddy, do fire ants get mad when you poke their nests with a stick?"

"Yes, Son. They want to devour anything that disturbs them. Why do you ask? *Yeeeeooooowwww!*"

"*Whew*, Daddy, those ants are really mad at you. Look at them crawling all over you. Do they hurt bad? I didn't know you could dance. Daddy, be quiet. You are scaring all the animals away."

"Let's get out of here while I still have some skin on my legs and hair on my head. Come on, Daniel. Come on, Daniel. Come on, Daniel. I really don't think you need another decomposing acorn treasure in your pocket."

We headed down a wide path. "Daniel, walk on this side. There's a small puddle over there on the far edge. It's getting chilly. Don't go near the…" *splash!* "…puddle."

"Sorry, Daddy. I couldn't get out of the way."

"How could you *not* have gotten out of the way? Did that puddle jump up and slap you? You were on the other side of the path and had to cross over a fallen log, squeeze between two trees, and cross ten feet of barren ground before you even came close to the puddle."

"I don't know. It just came out of nowhere. I won't…" *Splash!* "…do it again." *Splash, splash!*

"O.K., let's go." *Swish, swish, slop, slop.* "Daniel, how much water is in your boots? Did you leave any water in the puddle?"

A few feet farther down the trail, I was certain a bear had jumped from a tree.

"*Yeeee-hawww!* This is fun! Little trees make good swings." Daniel was bending over saplings to catapult himself through the air.

"Daniel, watch out. Some of those saplings don't look too strong. You might—" *Crack.* "Ouch! Break one."

"Daddy, that was fun. Can I do it again? Why do you look so silly?"

"I always look this way when I've been clobbered on the head with flying chunks of tree. Don't worry. That lump rising on my head will go away eventually; I'm almost certain."

And then, just as we neared a place loaded with game sign...

"Daddy, can we go now? I'm tired and cold. Carry me back to the truck."

"*Carry you?* Are you kidding? Your boots alone weigh another ton with all that slimy mud cemented on them. Maybe you should leave some of that dirt in the forest for next time."

It was two miles uphill back to the truck through rugged terrain: bramble thickets, swamps, ravines, and icy streams. I was carrying my gun, Daniel's BB gun, ammunition, water, fruit drinks, extra clothes, empty coffee jug, first-aid kit, and a ton of snacks.

"Besides, you are wet and dripping stinking goo from all the puddles you've 'accidentally' fallen into. You want me to carry you? I would have to be nuts."

It was a long hike back to my truck with Daniel on my shoulders. Upon arriving, I asked the most important parental question. "Do you have to potty? If so, do it now before I get you situated in the truck."

"No, I don't have to." I brushed off most of the dirt, took off his muddy boots, stripped him down to the last three layers to find reasonably clean, dry clothing, and hoisted him into the truck. *Click.* There is something about the sound of a seat belt fastening that causes a child's bladder to burst.

"I've got to go potty now and I can't wait."

I hoisted him from the truck, put his muddy boots and several layers of wet clothes back on, took the layers off so he could relieve himself, took his boots off, hoisted him back into the truck and secured the seat belt, again.

I'm not sure I've ever been so exhausted. I was quite sure I wouldn't be repeating this whole experience any time soon.

"Can we go again tomorrow, Daddy?"

Tomorrow?

"Of course, Son," I sighed, chuckling to myself. "I would love to."

John N. Felsher is a full-time freelance writer and photographer with more than 1,460 bylines in more than 100 magazines. He is also the national fishing writer for Examiner.com and the media specialist for Anglers Inn International (www.anglersinn.com). Contact him through his website, www.JohnNFelsher.com.

AMY LOU JENKINS

✳ ✳ ✳

Close to Home

Nature provides answers to life's hardest questions.

D.J. SPOTTED A DEER TRAIL THAT LOOKED AS IF IT LED TO the Menominee River while I tried to think of a way to explain death. This morning a buck with just an inch of antler crossed in front of our car, grabbing my line of sight with his intent dark eyes and reminding me that my eleven-year-old son and I were overdue for an outing. Nature came to get us. D.J. claimed the buck stared directly into his eyes as he passed, but I swore he glared into mine and even turned his head back over his shoulder to maintain eye contact as he traveled from parkway to suburban lawn. His interest in us evaporated as his front hooves hit the curb. We kept watching him, unaccustomed to seeing a slow-moving deer so near. Usually they bolt across our road or stand statuesque for a moment before darting back into the veil of trees and shrubs. This buck seized our attention and then became oblivious to us, as if we didn't exist in the same dimension.

July is the month the buck begins to regrow antlers in preparation to fight, to the death if needed, for the right to mate. His coat was caramel with cream trim, and scratched from shoulder to rear as if keyed by an angry hoodlum.

Although D.J. had seemed enthusiastic when he'd agreed to walk with me in our neighborhood woods, he raised his eyebrows as he saw me stuffing a backpack with bug repellent, water, and field guides to trees, birds, and wildflowers.

D.J.'s exploration with me was a gift he'd promised to give, and he didn't whine or try to beg off. Instead he teased, and before we'd left the yard he rapidly fired all the complaints he was too mature to say in earnest. "Are we almost home? How much farther? I have to go to the bathroom." That done, he elbowed me and pointed across the street to bright orange blooms of summer.

These day lily blossoms each last only one day and often bloom in succession. They are so prolific along roadsides, most folks call them ditch lilies. Six buds on a lily could mean that in six days the flowers would be gone for a year. Negative thinking, I told myself. Something else will come into bloom when the lilies are done, and more buds may form on these plants to bring more weeks of summer blossoms.

We crossed the blacktop road, and I silently recalled the mess we'd seen there on an evening dog walk last month. Perhaps D.J. did, too; his eyes focused on the same stretch of blacktop that revealed nothing of prior events, not even a faint stain. That night a possum lay split open on the street and seven nubs of babies crossed the road ahead of the body, recreating an image of the impact. D.J. had bent over one of the nubs, shook his head and ticked the roof of his mouth. The mamma and her scattered pearls were gone by morning.

There's a man in Milwaukee who drives an old truck under contract with the county and picks up offensive refuse that can be handled by one man: dead dogs, raccoons, and all manner of carrion and objects dumped on the street. I saw his picture in the paper a few autumns ago when he found a garbage bag holding a cold newborn baby with a smidgen of cry left in her. He called the Rescue Squad, and she lived. I wonder if now that man thinks of the baby girl, in a warm home, her light brown hair grown in. She's got to be walking, already talking like crazy, now almost ready for kindergarten. I wonder, as he scoops up death with his dark flat shovel, if he looks for life, if he turns his head and bends so that his ear grazes each found garbage bag and if he stops to weigh discarded parcels with his large worker hands, and if sometimes he tears open bags of litter dropped in arrogant thoughtlessness—just in case. I've never seen this man who works vampire hours, but I recall the strange reinterpretation of an American Gothic picture: man, upturned shovel, pickup truck.

His services may not be needed so close to our woods. Our small road kill is always gone by morning. When a deer dies, we have to call the DNR, and the carcass may sit a few days. For our smaller corpses, foxes slip out of their dens under cover of night, spill down the curb like quiet dark shadows and, with their sharp canines and incisors, drag the unsightly dead out of sight and into the woods we were about to enter.

We found a trail after crossing a secondary stream. We shoved and jostled, competing for the lead spot on the trail, which was too narrow to allow us to walk abreast. I took a wide step in front of D.J., cutting him off with my leg, and ran ahead. Low to the ground, I spotted two triangles of reddish tan fur. Ears, I thought, and a head, but the body flattened so the whole thing looked like a red fox rug lying askew on the forest floor, assuming the entire width of the trail. For a second I was fascinated, but then repulsed by busy maggot eyes and black carrion beetles feverishly animating the fur with their group undulations. Flies formed a buzzing helmet-like force field around the death. I realized I hadn't breathed and couldn't inhale. I ran backward on the trail, maneuvering

around D.J., and said, "Eeww, I don't want to be near it." I
didn't want to smell the rotten pungency, so I turned around.

He'd taken steps toward the carcass, closer than I'd been,
and stood transfixed at the consummation of this body. "Dad
and I found a deer in here last year, but it was just bones. It
wasn't gross like this fox."

I'd acted like a girl, and D.J. knew it was his job to be my
antonym. He calmly walked back to join me in the place I'd
found my breath.

"Mom, how do you think he died?"

"Don't know, but foxes in the wild only live about five
years. Usually they crawl back into their dens to die." I told
him what I knew, but not what he asked.

We pushed away the thick brush beneath a canopy of
maples and bur oak trees. The brush faded away and light di-
minished where a few immense gnarled trees created a room
with a ceiling of dense leaves and a floor of compact gray dirt
with hundreds of underground roots surfacing just enough to
create a shallow labyrinth. D.J. touched the furrowed bark of
the largest tree and asked what it was.

"Looks like a big old elm," I answered while searching the
backpack for my *Trees of Wisconsin* guide. While I searched the
tree book, D.J. poked my arm.

He nodded to a series of diminutive chalky batons scattered near the base of the tree, four bones from limbs and one
rib. "Too big for a squirrel. Maybe a groundhog."

We huddled and inspected the bones. D.J. spoke:
"Everything dies."

Right here is the place where I'm supposed to have the answers, I thought. I should give him the wisdom that will offer
comfort at my death and insight that he'll pass on to his children on a summer walk in decades to come.

As a nurse and daughter, I'd seen death. Two years earlier my stepfather, the man I called Pop, died from prostate cancer. Anomalous cells grew in his body. The aberrant proliferation killed him, and only then, by their own rampant quest to take over his body, did the cancer itself die.

Pop lived at our home most of the last six weeks before death. D.J. had passed his report card over the bars of the hospital bed to him, and played Christmas songs on his keyboard to cheer him up. Pop closed his eyes to listen and name the tunes:

"'O, Holy Night.' That's so beautiful."

"'We Three Kings.' I haven't heard that in years."

"'Silent Night.' That's tremendous, D.J., tremendous."

Like many cancer patients, Pop died in pieces: couldn't walk, couldn't stand, couldn't turn in bed, then nothing. In those last twenty-four hours, I'd given him a bedbath, and he moaned when I repositioned his gaunt body as gingerly as I knew how.

"Oh, Pop. I'm sorry."

"It's not you, it's me." He comforted me. "Just do what you need to do."

Pop died in his sleep that night, never losing the kindness and essence of who he was through the process. I gave a eulogy at Pop's funeral. I didn't then—nor later in the presence of that great tree—have anything momentous to say about the meaning of death. I could only tell the truth of how his love for life seemed to grow and mingle with his impending death.

A few hundred yards away from the tree and old bones, in the space I'd run away from, carrion beetles feasted on maggots born in the flesh of the fox. The entire forest is a composition of bits of organic matter that came from life feeding on death. Remnants of fox, tadpoles, wild geraniums, and trout lilies had perhaps cycled through the people who lived near this place. The body recycles its elements at different rates, but about every decade each atom of a body that is a part of living tissue is replaced. Every element that passed out of my body in the form of my son is now in use elsewhere. He follows the patterns of his own DNA blended from his parents, but the organs, cells, and atoms have all formed anew from reclaimed oddments of life and death.

As soon as that fox died, *E. coli* and other organisms already present in its gut proliferated in the hypoxic and acidic environment. The gut burst and spread the feeding organisms to the rest of the corpse. Bacterial and fungal parents engendered hundreds of generations of offspring in a few days. Yellow jackets, flies, and earthworms shared the bounty of the life-giving putrefaction and began new families. Soil mites, nematodes, and nitrogen-fixing bacteria moved into the fox's rich neighborhood. As many as a trillion live cells reside in one cubic centimeter of soil near decomposing remains.

"Everything dies," D.J. had said, but I hadn't responded and couldn't even determine if it was the life or death at the site of the dead fox that had repelled me.

All I'd discovered was that the tree wasn't an American elm. The living tree was an easier subject to discern. Its location near water and reddish tint in the furrows of the rough bark revealed it was a slippery elm.

D.J. started toward a deer trail, touching the trunks of trees with alternate hands, identifying the ones he knew: sugar maple, black willow, green ash, oak. Our path led to the edge of the water, then to the point where we'd had to climb out of the low riverbed to cross a bridge back into a neighborhood of houses, cars, and health walkers. A man in 1970-style running shorts walked in front of us smoking a cigarette. D.J. quietly laughed at his shorts and his hyperexposed boiled-egg-white thighs bizarrely antithetical to the coverage of the long baggy shorts that were currently the style. The cigarette smoke reached up through my nose to my brain to pull open a file drawer and summon the face of a patient I cared for when I was a new nurse. I'd seen her face hundreds of times. Her hungry eyes searched for a comfort that came only when her breathing stopped. I told D.J. about this first patient I ever cared for during a death—how she squeezed my hand, pinching my fingers into a tight bundle as she labored to breathe. Her family smoked in the waiting room, waiting for their matriarch to die of lung cancer. Despite high doses of intravenous analgesic and anti-anxiety medication, my patient struggled through her last breaths. Sitting erect, she reached for air as the cancer nicked off blood vessels and filled each of her alveoli with blood until there were no little air sacs left with a surface that could exchange carbon dioxide for oxygen. She drowned in her own blood as she clutched my hand. Seconds before I closed her wide-open eyes, an image of her face filed itself in my head. The smoky smell of the waiting room, where I announced her death, labeled the file.

D.J. recognized the anti-smoking agenda in my tale and diverted me by pulling me back into the undeveloped space along the river. A stand of prairie grass on a hill above the river was dotted with sweet pea vines and greeted us with a baby fresh scent. An expanse of mowed grasses between a lagoon and river let us walk abreast. D.J. hung his elbow around my shoulder and leaned on me while we walked.

We walked silently until D.J. blurted, "I believe in heaven and earth, and I think, I hope, we get to live forever."

This was my second opportunity to say something deep. "Jesus is our Savior, and because we believe in him we do have everlasting life."

He huffed. My response—too scripted for him. My neck hurt where the crook of his elbow tugged.

He said nothing.

I grew quiet again. Thoughts of death lead to God, because we must find a way to make peace with the end of life. The minister and writer F. Forrester Church said, "Religion is the human response to being alive and having to die." I'd been exploring Unitarianism and was attracted to the faith's searching for spiritual truths in Christianity, Judaism, nature, and eastern religions. I hadn't decided if my worshiping with Unitarians was an insult to my religious roots or a bridge between Christianity and openness to a spirituality not tied to dogma. The search felt right, even without a conclusion.

A large gray-blue "S" caught my eye in the lagoon. We stopped and turned while D.J. kept his arm on my shoulder. The bed of the lagoon heaved with polliwogs and crayfish. A great blue heron stalked. Stab, toss, catch, swallow. A graceful maneuver carried out with such adeptness we waited only a few minutes to see a replay of this death feeding life, judged beautiful.

On the way home we stopped at the Burleigh Bridge, where five willows along the side of the river reached for their own apparition. D.J. stared out into the river and spoke, "Mom, I do believe in God and life after death. I just don't know what that life will be." I don't know if Grandpa Paul went away to heaven; sometimes I think I feel him with us."

"Do you feel him now?" I asked.

D.J.'s pensive profile showed eyebrows, bushier than I remembered. His nose had grown out of the pug stage that mine never left. "The woods felt so busy today, like we were not alone."

"I felt it too," I said. It was like all of our ancestors and all those that lived before us came for a July reunion.

D.J. stared at the river. He wasn't looking at me; he wasn't looking to me. "Everything dies," D.J. told me.

It wasn't a question; it was an acknowledgment.

Amy Lou Jenkins holds an MFA in Literature and Creative Writing from Bennington College. Her first book Every Natural Fact: Five Seasons of Open-Air Parenting *will be released in 2010. Her work has appeared in* Earth Island Journal, The Florida Review, Flint Hills Review, Grit, Rosebud, *and many more. She teaches writing at workshops and as a guest lecturer/adjunct at various Midwest colleges. Find her online at www.AmyLouJenkins.com.*

DIANE SELKIRK

The Reluctant Adventurer

Only a toddler would stop in the snow to smell the roses.

THE SNOW LINE WAS HALFWAY DOWN THE MOUNTAIN. It looked as though a house painter had drawn a clear unwavering line that divided the green foliage from the new snow. The winter sky was a bright, inviting crystal blue; it was the sort of day I dream about during gray winter months.

"That is where we're going," I told two-and-a-half-year-old Maia as I pointed high up at the snowy peaks.

"Maybe make snow angels and toboggan ride?" she asked.

"No, this time we are going cross-country skiing. Remember the little skis we got?"

Maia chattered happily about her skis while my thoughts drifted to past ski trips with my husband. I recalled the pain in my tired legs and my snow-chilled hands the time we pushed on through bad weather in hope of shelter, and then how we crawled, half-frozen and hungry, from our tent after a fitful night to be welcomed by one of the most awesome vistas I'd seen in my life. The adventure was worth the pain, and maybe even sweeter because of it. Now that Maia has joined our life, I've missed hiking, kayaking, diving, and ski trips. We have gone on a few modified backpacking trips and done some car camping with Maia, but like leisurely Sunday brunches and wine-soaked late night debates with friends, high adventure seemed a pleasure of the past.

Maia joyfully clutched her tiny skis to her chest, and I felt a pang. Her cheeks were flushed with rosy excitement and she was sweetly bundled in multi-colored ski clothes. In that moment I wasn't entirely sure if I was mourning the adventurous life I once led, or celebrating the introduction of my daughter into an adventure-filled life of her own.

On the mountain, Maia lasted for ten minutes on her skis then demanded to go home. "We have more skiing to do," I coaxed. "If you are done skiing on your own, you can ride in the backpack on Daddy's back. We'll ski for a while then go to the ski lodge for a snack." At the offer of a snack Maia brightened and insisted we go to the lodge "right now!"

Feeling discouraged, we agreed to head for the lodge. I'd had a different vision for the day: we were going to ski hard, enjoy the view, then finish off with hot chocolate to celebrate our first great family skiing adventure. Instead, my daughter wanted to go home, play in the lodge, or throw snowballs—anything but ski.

Once we were on our way, Maia stopped complaining. My skis found their rhythm as the trees blurred and the rolling hills lulled me, and I wished the day would last forever. At the junction to the lodge I made eye contact with my husband Evan and we veered the other way. Silently we continued for another minute and a half. Then Maia started asking about the lodge.

"It's actually very far away," I lied with a twinge of guilt. "Why don't you pass the time by looking in the woods for some animals?" And so we skied a few trails while Maia reported sighting deer, squirrel, panthers, and gorillas, then what she adamantly insisted was the lodge. Stopping to look, we saw nothing but a trail leading into the woods.

"A trail would make a good adventure," Maia suggested. Reluctantly, I took off my skis. Evan freed her from the backpack, and we set off into the woods on foot.

I was not cheerful. Again, I was thinking about all the great things I used to do and how we now had to modify them beyond recognition. Maia was happy, though, as she set off on her escapade. She made her way through drifts, up and down hills, and over a snow bridge. Everything intrigued her; she examined footprints, peered in a frozen creek, and tested the flavor of the snow from several different patches.

Busy with my own sullen thoughts I hardly noticed when she stopped and stared at a bush. From just under the bush a little brown bunny stared back. Maia began talking to the bunny, too softly for me to hear, but with an intensity that made me keep quiet. Curious, I moved closer and heard Maia ask the bunny about Easter eggs, then give her name and a rough approximation of our address.

"We need to go now," Maia whispered to us. "She has to make chocolate eggs for so many kids."

Enchanted, we started back toward our skis. On the walk back, I joined in the adventure; we leaped over a creek, slid down a snow bank, and examined the chewed branches of a bush. Back at our skis Maia willingly got into the backpack and we skied for a while longer. She told us that seeing the Easter Bunny needed to be our secret, so other people wouldn't disturb her.

"She was my special adventure," Maia explained.

At the lodge, sipping hot chocolate, I was surprised to find myself feeling tired and content. Somewhere in that afternoon I realized that adventure comes not with what I do, but with how I receive it. I have happily exchanged sleeping in and reading the morning paper for being awakened too early by musical giggles. Spending the evening reading stories then nursing my daughter to sleep is every bit as meaningful to me as debating world events. I can miss what I had, but I owe it to myself—and Maia—to appreciate the beauty of what I have.

My family is my adventure. Our travels may not be the stuff of epic adventure tales or enticing articles anymore; our experiences are smaller, more personal, and I now realize, deeply fulfilling.

Raising my cup of hot chocolate, I proposed a toast: "To our first great family skiing adventure!"

"And," whispered Maia, "the Easter Bunny."

Diane Selkirk has continued to search for adventures to share with Maia and her husband Evan. The family recently set off aboard their forty-foot sailboat Ceilydh *on the first leg of a long-term, offshore sailing trip.*

DAVID GESSNER

Learning to Surf

Because stability just might be overrated.

OUT JUST BEYOND THE BREAKING WAVES THEY SIT THERE
bobbing, two groups of animals, avian and human, pelicans
and surfers. As they rise and fall on humps of water, the pelicans look entirely unperturbed, their foot-long bills pulled like
blades into scabbards, fitting like species-wide puzzle pieces
into the curves of their throats. The surfers, mostly kids, look
equally casual. A girl lies supine on her board, looking up at
the sky, one leg crossed over the other in an almost exaggerated posture of relaxation. For the most part the birds and
surfers ignore each other, rising up and dropping down together as the whole ocean heaves and then sighs.

Pelicans are particularly buoyant birds and they bob high
on the water as the surfers paddle and shift in anticipation.
There is no mistaking that this is the relatively tense calm of
before, rest before exertion. Soon the waves pick up and the
kids paddle furiously, gaining enough speed to pop up and
ride the crests of breaking surf. They glide in toward the beach
where I stand, the better ones carving the water and ducking
under and cutting back up through the waves.

I just recently moved to this North Carolina island town, but I have been here long enough to know that those who pursue this sport are guided by a kind of laid-back monomania. Each morning I bring my four-month-old daughter down to the local coffee shop, and each morning the talk is of one thing. The ocean, I've learned, is always referred to as *it*.

"What did it look like this morning?" one surfer asked another a few mornings back.

"Sloppy."

Remembering my own early-morning glance at the water I could understand what he meant, the way a series of waves came from the northwest, while another group muscled up from the south, and how the two collided and kicked up. Aesthetically it was beautiful, but practically, at least from a surfer's point of view, it made for a landscape of chop—not much to get excited about.

Another morning I heard this: "How does it look today, dude?"

"Small."

"Nothing?"

"You can go out there if you want to build your morale."

It's easy enough to laugh at these kids, but I like the physical nature of their obsession, the way their lives center on being strong animals. In *When Elephants Weep*, Jeffrey Masson speculates that animals feel *funktionslust*, a German word meaning "pleasure taken in what one can do best." The strongest of the surfers, the ones who have grown up on the waves, must certainly feel this animal pleasure as they glide over and weave through the water.

I watch the surfers for a while longer, but when the pelicans lift off I turn my focus toward their even more impressive athletic feats. Pelicans are huge and heavy birds, and the initial liftoff, as they turn into the wind and flap hard, is awkward. But once in the air they are all grace. They pull in their feet like landing gear and glide low between the troughs of the waves, then lift up to look for fish, flapping several times before coasting. If you watch them enough, a rhythm reveals itself: effort, *glide*, effort, *glide*. They are looking for small fish— menhaden or mullet most likely—and when they find what they are searching for they gauge the depth of the fish, and therefore the necessary height of the dive, a gauging guided by both instinct and experience. Then they pause, lift, measure again, and finally, plunge. The birds bank and twist and plummet, following their divining-rod bills toward the water. A few of them even turn in the air in a way that gives the impression they are showing off. If they were awkward in takeoff, now they are glorious.

There is something symphonic about the way the group hits the water, one bird after another: *thwuck, thwuck, thwuck.* At the last second before contact they become feathery arrows, thrusting their legs and wings backward and flattening their gular pouches. They are not tidy like terns and show no concern for the Olympian aesthetics of a small splash, hitting the surface with what looks like something close to recklessness. As soon as they strike the water, instinct triggers the opening of the huge pouch, and it umbrellas out, usually capturing fish, plural. While still underwater they turn again, often 180 degrees, so that when they emerge they'll be facing into the wind for takeoff. And when they pop back up barely a second later, they almost instantly assume a sitting posture on the water, once again bobbing peacefully. It's a little like watching a man serve a tennis ball who then, after the follow through, hops immediately into a La-Z-Boy.

The pelicans calm me, which is good. I have tried to maintain a relaxed attitude since moving to this island, but at times it's hard. I had vowed that I would stay forever on Cape Cod, my old home, but it was my writing about how much I loved the Cape that led to the offer of a teaching job in this over-crowded North Carolina resort town of outboard motors, condos, and southern accents. My wife, Nina, had just given birth to our daughter, Hadley, and the lure of health insurance and a steady paycheck was irresistible.

The truth is, the move has unsettled me: in coming to this new place I find myself, and my confidence, getting shaky. If I've behaved well publicly, in the privacy of our new apart-ment I've at times started to fall apart. As each day unfolds, I grow ever less sure of myself.

One of the things that disorients me is the heat. It's the kind of heat that makes you want to lie down and give up, to start to cry and throw out your arms in surrender. I've known brutal cold in my life, but cold has the advantage of invigora-tion, at least initially. Now I understand the logic behind sies-tas; every instinct tells you to crawl to a cool dank place and lie there and be still.

Lifting my daughter into our un-air-conditioned Honda Civic feels like sliding her into a kiln, so we are desperately trying to buy a new car. But today the Toyota guy calls with bad news. Our credit report has come back and our loan has been rejected.

"You have weak stability," he tells me, reading from the re-port.

I nod and consider the poetry of his words.

But there are other moments, moments when I sense that this may not be such a bad place to live. With summer end-ing, the parking lots have begun to empty. There are fewer beach walkers and more pelicans. Each morning I take long walks with Hadley, and have begun to take field notes on my daughter. I'm struck daily by her creatureliness, and the fact that this squirming little apelike animal, barely two feet high, has somehow been allowed to live in the same house with us.

Nothing cuts through my doubts about having moved here quite like this new ritual of walking with my daughter in a papooselike contraption on my chest. On good days we make it all the way to the south end of the island where we stare out at the channel.

Many things have caught me off guard about being a father, but the most startling thing has been the sheer animal pleasure. "Joy is the symptom by which right conduct is measured," wrote Joseph Wood Krutch of Thoreau. If that's true then my conduct these days must be excellent.

This morning we watch two immature, first-year pelicans fly right over the waves, belly to belly with their shadows. It's exhilarating the way they lift up together and sink down again, rollercoastering, their wings nicking the crests of the waves. Eight more adult birds skim right through the valley between the waves, gliding by the surfers, sweeping upward before plopping onto the water.

Feeling that it's only polite to get to know my new neighbors, I've begun to read about the birds. I've learned that the reason they fly through the troughs between the waves is to cut down on wind resistance, which means they, like the surfers they fly past, are unintentional physicists. When I first started watching pelicans I kept waiting to hear their calls, expecting a kind of loud *quack-quork*, like a cross between a raven and a duck. But my books confirm what I have already noticed, that adult pelicans go through their lives as near mutes. Whether perched atop a piling in classic silhouette or crossing bills with a mate or bobbing in the surf, they remain silent.

Another group of adult birds heads out to the west, toward the channel, as Hadley and I turn home. Before moving here

I never knew that pelicans flew in formations. They are not quite as orderly as geese—their Vs always slightly out of whack—and the sight of them is strange and startling to someone from the North. Each individual takes a turn at the head of the V, since the lead bird exerts the most effort and energy while the birds that follow draft the leader like bike racers. These platoons fly overhead at all hours of day, appearing so obviously prehistoric that it seems odd to me that people barely glance up, like ignoring an overflight of pterodactyls.

Yesterday I saw a bird point its great bill at the sky and then open its mouth until it seemed to almost invert its pouch. My reading informs me that these exercises are common, a way to stretch out the distensible gular pouch so that it maintains elasticity. Even more impressive, I learn that the pouch, when filled, can hold up to twenty-one pints—seventeen and a half pounds—of water.

"I have had a lifelong love affair with terns," wrote my friend from Cape Cod, John Hay, a writer whom I have always admired for his sense of rootedness. I've come to pelicans late and so can't have my own lifelong affair. But I am developing something of a crush.

I'm not a good watcher. Well, that's not exactly true. I'm a pretty good watcher. It's just that sooner or later I need to do more than watch. So today I am floating awkwardly on my neighbor Matt's surfboard, paddling with my legs in a frantic eggbeater motion, attempting this new sport in this new place while keeping one eye on the pelicans. Even though you can't bring your binoculars, it turns out that this is a great way to birdwatch. The pelicans fly close to my board, and for the first time I understand how enormous they are. I've read that they are fifty inches from bill to toe, and have six-and-a-half-foot wingspans, but these numbers don't convey the heft of their presence. One bird lands next to me and sits on the water, tucking its ancient bill into its throat. Up close its layered feathers look very unfeatherlike, more like strips of petrified wood. I watch it bob effortlessly in the choppy ocean. Most birds with webbed feet have three toes, but brown pelicans have four, and their webbing is especially thick. While this makes for awkward waddling on land, it also accounts for how comfortable the birds look in the water.

I'm not nearly as comfortable. Two days ago I spent an hour out here with Matt, and yesterday we came out again. Despite his patience and coaching, I never stood up on my board, in fact I never made more than the most spastic attempts. Today has been no better. The best things about surfing so far are watching the birds and the way my body feels afterward when I am scalding myself in our outdoor shower. So it is with some surprise that I find myself staring back with anticipation as a series of good waves roll in, and it is with something close to shock that I find myself suddenly, mysteriously, riding on top of that one perfect (in my case, very small) wave. Before I have time to think I realize that I am standing, actually standing up and surfing. The next second I am thrown into the waves and smashed about.

But that is enough to get a taste for it.

The human brain is no match for depression, for the chaos of uprootedness. To try to turn our brains on ourselves, to think we can solve our own problems within ourselves, is to get lost in a hall of mirrors. But there is a world beyond the human world and that is a reason for hope. From a very selfish human perspective, we need more than the human.

Water and birds have always helped me live, have always lifted me beyond myself, and this morning I paddle out beyond the breakers and lie with my back to the surfboard just like the girl I saw in early fall. But while my legs may be crossed casually, I spend most of the time worrying about falling off. Even so, as I bob up and down on the waves, the whole ocean lifting and dropping below me, my niggling mind does quiet for a minute. And then it goes beyond quiet. I'm thinking of Hadley, sitting up now and holding her own bottle, and I feel my chest fill with the joy these small achievements bring. She will be a strong girl I suspect, an athlete. And, no doubt, if we stay here she will become a surfer, delighting in her own *funktionslust*.

Glancing up at the pelicans flying overhead, I notice that there is something slightly backward-leaning about their posture, particularly when they are searching for fish, as if they were peering over spectacles. From directly below they look like giant kingfishers. But when they pull in their wings they change entirely: a prehistoric Bat Signal shining over Gotham. Then I see one bird with tattered feathers whose feet splay out crazily before he tucks to dive. When he tucks, dignity is regained, and the bird shoots into the water like a spear.

Inspired by that bird, I decide to turn my attention back to surfing. I catch a few waves, but catch them late, and so keep popping wheelies and being thrown off the surfboard. Then, after a while, I remember Matt telling me that I've been putting my weight too far back on the board. So on the next wave, almost without thinking, I shift my weight forward and pop right up. What surprises me most is how easy it is. I had allotted months for this advancement, but here I am, flying in toward the beach on top of a wave, its energy surging below.

A wild giddiness fills me. It's cliché to say that I am completely in the present moment as this happens, and it's also not really true. Halfway to shore I'm already imagining telling Nina about my great success, and near the end of my ride, as the great wave deposits me in knee-deep water, I find myself singing the *Hawaii Five-0* theme song right out loud.

Though no one is around I let out a little hoot, and by the time I jump off the board I'm laughing out loud. A week ago I watched some kids, who couldn't have been older than twelve or thirteen, as they ran down the beach on a Friday afternoon. Happy that school was out, they sprinted into the water before diving onto their boards and gliding into the froth of surf. I'm not sprinting, but I do turn around and walk the surfboard back out until I am hip deep, momentarily happy to be the animal I am, my whole self buzzing from a ride that has been more the result of grace than effort. Then, still laughing a little, I climb on top of the board and paddle back into the waves.

I could end on that note of grace, but it wouldn't be entirely accurate. The year doesn't conclude triumphantly with me astride the board, trumpets blaring, as I ride that great wave to shore. Instead it moves forward in the quotidian way years do, extending deep into winter and then once again opening up into spring. As the days pass, my new place becomes less new, and the sight of the squadrons of pelicans loses some of its thrill. This too is perfectly natural, a process known in biology as habituation. Among both birds and humans, habituation is, according to my books, the "gradual reduction in the strength of a response due to repetitive stimulation." This is a fancy way of saying we get used to things.

While the pelican brain repeats ancient patterns, the human brain feeds on the new. On a biological level novelty is vital to the human experience: at birth the human brain is wired so that it is attracted to the unfamiliar. I see this in my daughter as she begins to conduct more sophisticated experiments in the physical world. True, all of these experiments end the same way, with her putting the object of experimentation into her mouth, but soon enough she will move on to more sophisticated interactions with her environment. She's already beginning to attempt language and locomotion. Although pelicans her age are already diving for fish, she, as a *Homo sapiens,* can afford to spot *Pelecanus occidentalis* a lead. She will gain ground later. Her long primate infancy will allow her relatively enormous brain to develop in ways that are as foreign to the birds as their simplicity is to us, and will allow that brain to fly to places the birds can never reach.

While I acknowledge these vast differences between bird and human, there is something fundamentally unifying in the two experiences of watching the pelicans and watching my daughter. There is a sense that both experiences help me fulfill Emerson's still-vital dictum: "First, be a good animal." For me fatherhood has intensified the possibility of loss, the sense that we live in a world of weak stability. But it has also given me a more direct connection to my animal self, and so, in the face of the world's chaos, I try to be a good animal. I get out on the water in an attempt to live closer to what the nature writer Henry Beston called "an elemental life."

I keep surfing into late fall, actually getting up a few times. But then one day I abruptly quit. On that day it is big, much too big for a beginner like me. I should understand this when I have trouble paddling out, the waves looming above me before throwing my board and self backward. And I should understand this as I wait to catch waves, the watery world lifting me higher than ever before. But despite the quiet voice that is telling me to go home I give it a try, and before I know it I am racing forward, triumphant and exhilarated, until the tip of my board dips under and the wave bullies into me from behind and I am thrown, rag-doll style, and held under by the wave. Then I'm tossed forward again and the board, tethered to my foot by a safety strap, recoils and slams into my head. I do not black out; I emerge and stagger to the shore, touching my hand to the blood and sand on my face. The next night I teach my Forms of Creative Nonfiction class with a black eye.

So that is enough, you see. One of the new territories I am entering is that of middle age, and the world doesn't need too many middle-aged surfers.

I feared fatherhood, but most of the results of procreation have been delightful ones. One exception, however, is the way that disaster seems to loom around every corner—disaster that might befall my daughter, my wife, myself. No sense adding "death by surfing" to the list.

While I have naturally begun to take the pelicans for granted, they still provide daily pleasures throughout the winter. What I lose in novelty, I gain in the early stages of intimacy. I see them everywhere: as I commute to work they fly low in front of my windshield; they placidly perch atop the pilings while I sip my evening beer on the dock near our house; they bank above me as I drive over the drawbridge to town. My research reveals that in March they begin their annual ritual of mating: a male offers the female a twig for nest-building and then, if she accepts, they bow to each other before embarking on the less elegant aspect of the ritual, the actual mating, which lasts no more than twenty seconds. These rituals are taking place, as they should, in privacy, twenty miles south on a tiny island in the mouth of the Cape Fear River. The eggs are laid in late March or early April and a month-long period of incubation begins.

Around the midpoint of incubation, my human family achieves its own milestone. Throughout the spring I have continued to carry my daughter down the beach to watch the pelicans fish, but today is different from the other days. Today Hadley no longer rests in a pouch on my chest but walks beside me hand in hand.

I remind myself that the mushiness I feel at this moment, the sensation that some describe as sentimentality, also serves an evolutionary purpose. With that softening comes a fierceness, a fierce need to protect and aid and sacrifice. This is not a theoretical thing but a biological one. In fact this transformation borders the savage, and here too the pelicans have long served humans as myth and symbol. "I am like a pelican of the wilderness," reads Psalm 102. At some point early Christians got it into their heads that pelicans fed their young with the blood from their own breasts, a mistake perhaps based on the red at the tip of some pelican bills, or, less plausibly, on their habit of regurgitating their fishy meals for their young. Whatever the roots of this misapprehension, the birds became a symbol of both parental sacrifice and, on a grander scale, of Christ's own sacrifice. The images of pelicans as self-stabbing birds, turning on their own chests with their bills, were carved in stone and wood and still adorn churches all over Europe. Later, the parental symbol was sometimes reversed, so that Lear, railing against his famous ingrate offspring, calls them "those pelican daughters."

The year culminates in a single day, a day full of green, each tree and bird defined sharply as if with silver edges. I kiss Nina and Hadley goodbye while they are still asleep and head out at dawn to the road where Walker will pick me up. Walker Golder is the deputy director of the North Carolina Audubon Society, a friend of a new friend, and today he takes me in a small outboard down to the islands at the mouth of the Cape Fear River. We bomb through a man-made canal called

Snow's Cut and I smile stupidly at the clarity of the colors: the blue water, the brown eroding banks, the green above.

We stop at four islands. The southernmost of these is filled with ibis nests—11,504 to be exact. Ten percent of North America's ibises begin their lives here, and at one point we stand amid a snowy blizzard of birds, vivid white plumage and flaming bills swirling around us. Next we visit an island of terns, the whole colony seemingly in an irritable mood. This island, and its nearby twin, were formed when the river was dredged in the '70s by the U.S. Army Corps of Engineers, which used the sand to consciously aid the Audubon Society in an attempt to create nesting grounds. Terns, like ibises and pelicans, require isolated breeding areas, preferably islands, and this human experiment, this marriage of birders and engineers, has worked to perfection. We watch as a pair of royal terns spiral above us in their courtship dance.

The terns are impressive, but the highlight of the day for me is North Pelican Island, the nesting ground of almost all of the pelicans I have watched over the last year. Hundreds of pelicans sit on their ground nests, some of which are as big as beanbag chairs. They watch impassively as we approach. The old naturalists might have called these birds "undemonstrative" and "lugubrious," but I'll go with "calm." In fact, while we're anthropomorphizing, I might as well put "Buddha-like" in front of calm. It's hard not to project this on them after experiencing the wild defensiveness of the tern colony. The pelicans barely glance up at us. Theirs is a much different survival strategy, a much quieter one, but natural for such a big bird with no native predators on these islands. I crunch up through the marsh elder and phragmites to a spot where two hundred or so pelicans are packed together, sitting on their nests, incubating. Some still have the rich chestnut patches on the backs of their heads and necks, a delightful chocolate brown: leftover breeding plumage. They sit in what I now recognize as their characteristic manner, swordlike bills tucked into the fronts of their long necks.

While the birds remain quiet and calm, there is a sense of urgency here. This marsh island, like most of the islands that pelicans breed on, is very close to sea level. One moon-tide storm could wash over it and drown the season out. It is a time of year marked both by wild hope and wild precariousness, danger and growth going hand-in-hand. The birds are never more vulnerable, and as a father, I know the feeling.

I'm not sure exactly what I gain from intertwining my own life with the lives of the animals I live near, but I enjoy it on a purely physical level. Maybe I hope that some of this calm, this sense of ritual, will be contagious. If the pelicans look lugubrious to some, their effect on me is anything but. And so I indulge myself for a moment and allow myself to feel unity with the ancient birds. It may sound trite to say that we are all brothers and sisters, all united, but it is also simply and biologically true. DNA undermines the myth of our species' uniqueness, and you don't need a science degree to reach this conclusion. We are animals, and when we pretend we are something better, we become something worse.

Having seen these fragile nesting grounds a thousand times before, Walker is to some extent habituated to them. He is also more responsible than any other human being for their protection. "We only visit briefly in the cool of the morning," he explains, "so not to disturb the birds." Playing tour guide, he walks in closer to the nests and gestures for me to follow. He points to some eggs that look anything but lusterless, and then to another nest where we see two birds, each just a day old. Though pelicans develop quickly, they are born featherless and blind, completely dependent on their parents, their lives a wild gamble. Heat regulation, Walker explains, is a big factor in nestling survival. Pelican parents must shade their young on hot days, and one dog let loose on this island while the owner gets out of his boat to take a leak could drive the parents from the nest, resulting in the deaths of hundreds of nestlings.

But we are not thinking about death, not right now. We are instead watching these tiny purple dinosaurs that could ft in the palm of your hand, the beginnings of their extravagant bills already in embryonic evidence. And then, in a neighboring nest an egg trembles. There's a tapping, and a pipping out from within.

A small blind purple head emerges from the shell. "Something only a mother could love," Walker says, and we laugh. But we are both in awe. It is the beginning of something, any idiot can see that. But what may be harder to see is that it is also a great and epic continuation.

While we watch, the almost-pelican cracks through the eggshell, furious for life. Then it shakes off the bits of shell and steps out into a new and unknown world.

David Gessner is the author of several books, including Soaring with Fidel, The Prophet of Dry Hill, *and* Return of the Osprey, *which was chosen by the Boston Globe as one of the top ten nonfiction books of the year and the Book-of-the-Month club as one of its top books of the year.* The Globe *called it a "classic of American nature writing." In 2006 he won a Pushcart Prize. David has taught environmental writing at Harvard, and is currently an assistant professor at the University of North Carolina at Wilmington. He is the editor of the national literary journal,* Ecotone.

✦ ✦ ✦

Night Terrors

*"Grandma, I can't believe you rented us a cabin
that's, like, haunted!"*

A BLOOD-CURDLING SCREAM JARRED ME AWAKE. I LAY
perfectly still, pretending I was dead, just in case something
sinister was afoot. Besides, I couldn't have moved if I'd wanted
to—I was paralyzed with fear.

Suddenly something leaped on me. My heart ground to a
halt, my eyes rolled back into my head, and a death rattle
shuddered from my mouth.

Then…nothing.

"*GRANDMA!*" my teenage granddaughter Heather
yelled, shaking me. "Wake up! I'm scared; I think there's a
monster in the cabin."

"*You're* scared?" I gasped. "I just had a near-death experience hearing you scream. Did you have to *leap* on me?"

"Grandma, I'm serious; I'm really spooked."

"Tell me about it. I can't take this anymore; I'm getting too
old for this kind of excitement. This is the last vacation I take
with you grandkids."

"But, Grandma, I dreamed an animal was crawling on my
feet. I kicked it away, but then it landed on my chest. That's
when I screamed and threw it off, toward your bed."

"Thanks a lot," I said. "Seems we had the same nightmare. Except the rogue animal that jumped on me was *you*!"

Callie and Daidre, my other teen granddaughters, arrived at our cabin in the Wisconsin woods the next day, and when we told them about our strange nocturnal experience, Callie remarked, "That's so rad, you guys. I never dream."

But the following morning, as the four of us were getting ready for a swim in the lake, Daidre announced, "I had a really weird nightmare. An animal was crawling on me, trying to molest me."

Hearing this, the rest of us stopped and stared at Daidre, mouths gaping.

"Did I, like, say something weird?" Daidre asked.

"Yes!" we caroled.

I reminded her of Heather's dream and informed her that, coincidence aside, animals don't molest.

"Yeah, well, then why was it clawing at my chest?" she demanded.

We all had a good laugh, and then Heather asked, "What did your animal look like, Daidre?"

"I didn't care how it *looked*," Daidre flippantly declared. "All I know is that it was large, like a bobcat."

Later that day, I left the girls at the lake and went next door to talk to the cabin's owner. I asked her rather cryptically if an animal had ever died in the cabin where we were staying.

She frowned, concerned. "Is there a smell?"

"No, nothing like that. I was just wondering if, say, a possum might have died in there, in the past..."

"Well, two years ago a fairly large gray squirrel did get trapped in the cabin over the winter and died trying to claw its way out. My husband and I found it when we came back in spring. I can't imagine you'd still smell it, though."

That night, while we were sitting around playing cards, I

told my granddaughters what I had learned of our phantom animal.

"Grandma! I can't believe you rented us a place that's, like, *haunted,*" Callie moaned. "I want to go home!"

With that announcement, they all started screaming and hopping around, flapping their arms as if to brush away something icky.

"Stop screaming!" I yelled. "And settle down. You're too old to be acting like scaredy-cats."

Daidre, the youngest of them, came to her senses. "Grandma's right. Besides, the animal's, like, dead, so how can it hurt us?"

"Moreover," I sighed, "we can't go home. It's more than a four-hour ride, and I'm not driving in the dark."

To calm them down and take their minds off the spectral squirrel, I made some popcorn and pizza while we finished playing our card game. But at bedtime, the girls decided we should all sleep together in one room. Fortunately for me, they had worn themselves out with all of the silly talk and giggling, so they fell asleep as soon as they hit their pillows. I tossed and turned until I found a comfortable position and had just drifted off when I felt something leap at me in the dark. I frantically flung the bed blankets away, my heart beating at my chest as if trying to escape. The commotion woke the girls who then jumped screaming onto my bed, knocking the wind out of me.

Callie switched on the light and stared at me. "Grandma's dead. The ghost animal killed her!"

They ran helter-skelter from the cabin to the car, leaving me lying there. For a few seconds I wasn't sure if my body would get up on command. At my age, a body has a mind of its own. But apparently it wanted out of the cabin as much as

I did because I gave a lurch and sprang from the bed as spryly as the girls.

As we were driving away, Heather exclaimed, "Grandma, look back at the cabin window!"

We all looked back. In our haste to pack and evacuate we had left the lights on, and there, silhouetted in the window, was what looked like a gray squirrel—smiling.

In her thirty-year writing career, Sylvia Bright-Green has been published in nine anthologies, The Sheboygan County: 150 Years of Progress *and* Famous Wisconsin Mystics. *She has sold over 1,500 manuscripts to newspapers and magazines, and is actively involved in her state writers' organization.*

✦ ✦ ✦

The Adventures of John One-Eye

A pirate's treasure, lost and found.

"BACK LONG AGO IN THE DAYS WHEN I WAS A PIRATE," said my husband Michael, adjusting the bandana around his head, "I met a man named John One-Eye. He was old even then, and he told me about some treasure he hid in the forest. Do you want to come and look for it with me?" He knelt down under the tree where our son Rowan and his five-year-old friends sat spellbound.

The children's eyes widened with wonder. "Yes," they whispered.

Michael smiled and stood up. "Then come with me." He beckoned and eight children fell into line.

"Let's look under the cedars. Do you see anything there?" Michael bent low and crawled under the overhanging branches of a cedar tree. The children followed him into the clearing. They scurried around, peering over roots and under branches.

"Nothing here," said Rowan.

"Then we'll have to go farther along the trail."

I smiled and walked back to the picnic table to wait. I was glad for a few minutes to myself, to listen to the quiet of the park, and the noises of children having fun. I could hear them as they squealed in delight when Michael pretended to ask a duck if he had seen any treasure. They wandered along the path, searching among the salal and hostas and running in the grass just for the fun of it, until at last Michael led them to a stand of pines.

I set the picnic table with orange plastic birthday plates and blue cups. The sun was strong for an April morning. Not far off I heard, "Here it is! Here it is!" Rowan spied it first, but sixteen little hands reached upwards as Michael lowered the box down and pulled off the lid. Inside were cake and strawberries, and little goodie bags for each child.

The children gathered around the table. Their faces were flushed from running, and their hands stained red from strawberries. "Was your dad really a pirate?" said a small voice, muffled with cake.

"Yeah," Rowan nodded happily. Michael looked at me over the heads of the children and winked. And with that, a story was born.

It didn't take much for us to make John One-Eye come alive. Michael and I laughed together that evening, planning a wilderness adventure we could all enjoy.

"I hope he likes it," I mused.

"He'll love it," said Michael.

Rowan found the letter in the tree house one Saturday morning.

Dear Rowan,

Don't be surprised that I know your name. I have been keeping my eye on you since you were a small boy, and now I know that you are ready to take over where your dad left off.

The last time I saw your dad he said that he
would find the treasure for me when the time came.
The time is near. On the day before the next full
moon the X will mark the spot. Don't tell anyone but
your mum and dad.

Good Luck,
Pirate John One-Eye

There was a map of nearby China Beach, a pair of hiking
boots, and a backpack.

Rowan kept his secret proudly. He counted off the days.
Each night at bedtime he said to Michael, "Tell me more
about John One-Eye." And they would snuggle into bed
while Michael wove more and more detail into the story.

China Beach is an hour's drive from Victoria, B.C., along the
west coast of Vancouver Island. The Olympic Peninsula loomed
bright to our west, above the waters of the Juan de Fuca strait.

"Are we there yet?" asked Rowan at every strip of beach
we passed.

"Let's split up," he suggested as soon as we walked out of
the path onto China Beach. He took Michael by the arm and
led him along the eastern side of the beach. I jumped over the
creek and headed west. There is nothing like China Beach on
a sunny day. The surf rumbles as it washes over the stones, and
seals hide in the kelp beds just off shore. I could hear Rowan
squealing as Michael chased him along a sandy patch. They
found a long piece of kelp and pulled it behind them. Even
John One-Eye was forgotten for the moment.

There was a tall hollow stump partway down the beach,
with some logs crossed in front of it. X marks the spot.

"Yoo hoo," I called.

It only took a minute for Rowan to find the treasure.
"Look, look, there it is." He climbed up the stump and pulled

out the bag. Inside were gold covered chocolate coins, a silver chalice, a necklace of silver and pearls, and a ship's bell.

"Wow, real treasure," said Rowan. He laid each piece out carefully next to his kelp.

We spent the day lolling on the beach. Rowan collected rocks and made sand castles. Michael and I basked in the early sun. In the afternoon we walked to the end of the beach and spent a long time poking in tide pools.

"Look Mama, more treasures." Rowan pointed to the red sea anemones waving their fingers in the water.

When the tide came in over the tide pools we walked into the forest to a small waterfall in a tiny hidden cove.

"I wonder if John One-Eye ever hid in here," Rowan said.

"I'm sure he did," said Michael with a smile.

Back on the beach Rowan gathered his treasures: the coins, chalice, necklace, bell, rocks, and shells, and we headed home.

That fall Rowan started kindergarten. He learned about Sponge Bob and Yu Gi Oh cards. On the weekends he wanted to play with friends from school. But I kept the memory of our family adventure on the beach close, and when spring came around again, I wrote another letter.

Dear Rowan,

I have been entrusted with jewels from the house of the Shah of Oman. But spies are on to me, and I need to hide them. Will you look after them for me? Look for them at Mystic Beach next weekend. Hide them well. I'll let you know when the spies are gone and I can give them back to the Shah.

Thank you, Rowan.
John One-Eye

Rowan said, with a knowing look in his eye, "He needs us again Mama."

The walk down to Mystic Beach is through old-growth Douglas fir forest. It was quiet, except for the rush of a stream. There was a light mist in the air as the three of us walked hand-in-hand down the path. We listened to the cry of an eagle. It was a long walk for a six-year-old, but Rowan was caught in the dream of our adventure.

There was no time for a picnic before we set off to find the jewels. Rowan headed straight for a tall waterfall at the far end of the beach, as if he knew it was the right spot.

"Look, he's been here," he said.

I turned to follow him under the cascading waterfall into the cave behind. We laughed as the spray caught me. Rowan marched to the back of the cave and pointed. There in the corner was a stack of stones, carefully tucked away far from curious eyes.

"X marks the spot," he said.

As he dug I wandered around the little cave. In each crevice and on every shelf I found a small stack of stones or shells: someone's art, left behind for others to admire.

"Look Mama," Rowan returned to me with his hands and his pockets bulging. "I found tons of treasure." In his left hand he carried the tiny sack with jewels from John One-Eye. In his right, a sea urchin skeleton.

"What's in your pockets?"

"Stones." He carefully placed the jewels and sea urchin on a rock and pulled out smooth round stones from his pockets.

"Do you think all of those are from John One-Eye?" I asked.

"Oh no, those are pirate treasures," he said pointing to the sack of jewels. "And these are beach treasures."

"Aha," I said.

At that time of year the air was moist with salt and the green leaves reaching out to the beach from the forest dripped slowly. We sat under a tarp expertly raised by Michael, and watched the seagulls play. Rowan started us in a round of "Down by the Bay." When lunch was over Michael and Rowan walked to the water's edge to throw rocks in the waves. I was the first to see it: the blowing mist just past the kelp. Gray whales. Michael held Rowan up so he could see. The whales didn't care about the rain and the mist, and neither did we. We followed them as they made their way along the beach, breaching and blowing every so often, as if they were watching us, as we watched them.

Life got busy after that. Rowan started full-time school. There were music lessons and soccer. He and his friends talked about *Star Wars* and learned hockey statistics. I packed the costumes carefully away in a trunk. Michael and I were busy too, with work and the business of every day. But one morning in spring Rowan looked out at the tree house and said, "I wonder when John One-Eye will write again."

A few days later, he found a letter in the tree house.

Dear Rowan,

Please take the jewels to the lighthouse on Discovery Island. I will try to meet you there. The spies are gone, and it is now safe for me to give the Shah back his jewels. He is eager to have them back. If I don't make it, hide them well. Thank you for holding them all this time.

John One-Eye

We loaded up a big double kayak with gear and kayaked out to nearby Discovery Island. The sea was as calm as glass, and the boundary between sky and sea washed away in the rain. Rowan scanned the shore with his binoculars, searching for the lighthouse where we were to leave the treasure for John One-Eye.

We set up the tent by the edge of the beach, on a bluff. From there we could see back towards Victoria, and across the waters to Trial Island. The waves lapped the sand. Behind us a tall Garry Oak tree creaked under the weight of an angry crow.

When the tent was set, we took the kayak around the island to the lighthouse. A sailboat struggled in the eddy line of an offshore current.

"I wonder if that's John One-Eye's boat." Rowan looked thoughtful.

"You never know," said Michael, "but he might have got caught in the doldrums, or lost his way in the trade winds." He steered the kayak gently onto the beach.

We settled down on a step and opened our picnic.

"Look Mama," Rowan whispered. His finger pointed to a golden oriole fluttering among the shrubs. He handed me the binoculars, but the bird moved too quickly.

"I'm going to see if I can get closer." Like a cat, he crept towards the bird.

I leaned into Michael. "What a beautiful place this is."

When Rowan came back he said, "Look, that boat's not any closer." He was right. The strong current was forcing the boat away from the island. "Must be the trade winds," said Michael.

"Then we better hide the jewels," said Rowan. He chose a spot in a hollowed-out column, just under the lighthouse tower. He stuffed the jewels in tight.

"How come I've never met John One-Eye?" Rowan asked that evening in the tent.

"Well, I met him about twenty years ago," said Michael. "He was already 360 years old by then, because he had drunk from the spring of eternal life, but he was beginning to feel his age. He said it was hard for him to travel..." As Michael continued to build on the story I wondered about the time when we would have to tell Rowan that there was no John One-Eye. Santa Claus had already gracefully slipped away, the costume folded in the trunk and forgotten. I lay in the tent and remembered the beaches we had explored, the trips we had been on. I opened the tent door wider, to take in every detail so I would be able to remember it forever.

It was not long after that trip that Michael and I realized that Rowan was close to knowing the truth about John One-Eye. He found inconsistencies in the stories, which he pointed out. Michael said, "Oh, it's hard to remember, he told me so much," but Rowan was less and less easily convinced.

Just before Christmas, the year Rowan was eight, he received one last letter.

Dear Rowan,

This may be the last letter you get from me. I have tired of pirating, and am retiring to the Caribbean. I hope you can come and visit me some day. Thanks for all your help.

John One-Eye

Rowan closed the letter and looked me right in the eye. "Mum, are you John One-Eye?"

I thought of the years of John One-Eye and all the lessons I had learned. About the nature of treasure, about how to be lazy, about the beauty of make-believe. I knew I shouldn't lie, but I was so reluctant to let it end. The longer I was silent, the more he knew.

"Mum," he asked again. "*Are you?*"

"Yes," I said sadly.

He turned his head, to hide the tears in his eyes. He took a deep breath, "You lied. You lied."

This surprised me. He had let go of Santa Claus so easily, and his questions—my answers—about John One-Eye seemed so close to the truth. I wasn't prepared for this.

"Oh Rowan. We didn't mean to lie, we were telling a story. It was make-believe…" My voice trailed off.

He ran into his room to fight his disappointment alone.

I sat in the kitchen and grieved the innocence that had passed from our lives. For Michael and me those outings were a way to share in a child's simple pleasures: a rock, a shell, a make-believe. The story of John One-Eye had given us a way to let our imaginations soar together as a family.

A long time later Rowan came back out of his room, eyes red and puffy. His struggle had been hard.

"Mum," he said in a quiet voice, "does this mean we can't have John One-Eye anymore? Can he come again? Please?"

In his retirement in the Caribbean John One-Eye came across an egg which he believes may be the last of the silver fire dragons. Rowan is currently seeking possible rocky homes for the dragon once it hatches.

Kari Jones lives and writes in Victoria, B.C., where she and her family spend as much time as they can hiking, kayaking, and camping. She has written many articles on taking children into the great outdoors, and is co-author of a book titled Hiking Adventures with Children. *Kari believes that imagination is an important ingredient for a full life.*

MICHAEL QUINN PATTON

* * *

The Real Abyss

*Traversing the Grand Canyon, father and son share
in an unspoken rite of passage.*

BRANDON DISAPPEARED IN A HUGE SPLASH AND CAME UP
screaming, "Yowl! Youp! Yoweeee!" He thrashed about to gen-
erate warmth, swam over directly under the waterfall, played
under the falls, turned back and swam underwater, came up
for air, saw me and waved, went back under the water, and
started swimming back toward the boulder. I retreated so he
couldn't pull me in. From a safe distance I shouted, "I'll swim
after rock-lizard time. Enjoy."

I awoke in a midday mind fog, needing a second to remember where I was. I tried opening my eyelids. Even with
my hat over my eyes, the brightness hurt. I let them adjust for
a few seconds, then removed the hat and sat up. I saw Brandon
standing naked on the larger of the two boulders that blocked
the water's descent into the creek. From my vantage point,
slightly above and to the side, I could study him undetected,
his shoulder-length hair enveloping his face as he looked out
across the pool, his dark pubic hair providing contrast to his
wheat-colored body. His arms were folded across his chest and
he stood very still, peering into the water. Then, in a burst, he
leaped forward into the pool.

Rarely are we permitted, after toddlerhood, such unfettered moments of parental observation. Such an occasion cannot be planned any more than a spontaneous expression of love can be solicited.

I climbed down to join him. He came out gasping. "Ummmm, that feels good. It's deeeppp. I can't touch bottom anywhere." Then, he turned to the pool. "Sorry for disturbing your tranquility, fishies. Can't be selfish, though. Have to learn to share."

I undressed slowly, still groggy from my nap, then slipped into the water and retraced Brandon's invisible path, modestly emulating his shouts, induced involuntarily by the cold. My body reacted against the shock with a thermal charge that gave me a warm tingling throughout of heat in the midst of cold. I noticed with surprise and satisfaction that our swimming had no effect on the sparkling clearness of the water. I looked up from studying how the rock lined the pool just in time to get hit by the full force of a hard splash as Brandon jumped in again. I climbed out, my body feeling numb, drained, and, at last, detoxed.

We repeated this ritual several times. The cold would force us from the water, but the depths drew us back in. I finally yielded to the westerly origin of the sun's rays, alerting Brandon that we weren't leaving any margin for the unexpected during our descent. He insisted on one more cannonball, took a final turn under the waterfall, and climbed out.

Dressed, booted, and ready to take our leave, we stood together for a final look, close enough to touch arm to arm. Then we were off.

Late-afternoon shadows engulfed the gorge as we arrived back at the convergence of Merlin and Modred abysses. We continued on without pause or ceremony. The pace Brandon set matched my outer limit. I ignored messages from my legs screaming for a break, then dropped in relief beside Brandon when I found him stopped in an area thick with brush where a collapse in the Tapeats wall had dumped rocks along the bank. He had been watching for the place where we had descended that morning into Shinumo Creek from the Tonto Platform above. "Up or down?" he asked as I downed a swig of water.

We examined the map, saw we still had a long way to go, and considered our options. "It comes down to how adventurous we feel," I concluded.

"We know the Tonto route, but finding a way back down through the Tapeats will be tough, especially in the dark. We've been making good time down this gorge, but ahead lies unknown territory. It's your initiation. You make the call."

"It's probably faster hiking straight on down instead of going in and out around all the drainages on the Tonto. I'd just as soon keep going."

The first hint of trouble came where the creek dropped into a rocky gorge with smooth, slippery walls on both sides. We found just enough terracing on one side that by stepping slowly, foot over foot, and leaning in toward the wall, we made it, relieved not to fall into the cascading, waist-high water. Around the next turn we followed a narrow ledge under an overhang that ended at an impassable, inward-sloping wall. A midstream boulder pointed to an escape route across to the other side. From there we climbed a terraced series of ledges that led some fifteen feet up, over a precipice, down along a rapids, and around a small waterfall.

And so it went: hard, slow, tiring, but doable. We expected Shinumo to be joined by Flint Creek at any time, but instead the gorge just got narrower, the water deeper. We came to another small waterfall and rapids, negotiated a way around, and perched on two large boulders in the middle of the creek, marble smooth walls and overhangs on both sides. In front of us was a reservoir created by a massive boulder that dammed the gorge, leaving no route along either side. The only way forward was through the pool. In the flat, ebbing light we could not tell how deep it was nor how swift the current. The view beyond the boulder was restricted. So were our options.

My primary concern was not the thirty yards of water below us, but how many more such pools might lay ahead. We stripped, wadded our clothes in our t-shirts, tied our boots together, and arranged the clothes, boots, and hip packs so that the whole load could be carried over our heads. "Ready?" Brandon asked.

"It'll probably be slippery," I warned in reply, "so be prepared to swim. And if we're forced to let go of something, let's drop our clothes. Walking naked is easier than barefoot."

His grin told me he understood I was saying the things a parent feels compelled to say. His scream as he entered the frigid water cut off his effort at reassuring me. He dropped immediately into waist-high water, holding his boots and pack in one hand and the wad of clothes overhead in the other. As he pushed slowly forward, the water became chest-high, making it harder to brace against the current. He called back, "The bottom feels solid. The footing is fine."

Suddenly he was underwater. He dropped straight down, as if pulled by some submerged monster. I tensed, ready to jump in. A hand reappeared holding the boots. Then his head. He looked back as he gasped a breath. It looked like he wanted to call something back to me, but couldn't. He kicked forward, holding onto the things in his hands and letting me see the boots high overhead. Then, just as quickly as he had gone under, he had his footing again, the water chest-high, then waist-high, then he reached the other side, gasping for breath.

With the noise of the cascading water echoing in the gorge

I knew I wouldn't be able to hear him that far away. What could he tell me that I hadn't already seen? I slipped into the water, ready for the drop-off, so I went from walking to treading water without going under.

"Sorry about the boots," he said as I climbed out beside him, admonishing himself for failing to heed my one parental caution.

"Looked to me like you did well just hanging onto them." I stretched on tiptoes to peer around the boulder blocking our path. "We need to hurry. Let's get dressed and move. It can't be far to Flint now," I asserted, wondering if my lack of conviction showed.

Beyond the boulder we negotiated a ledge of sloping rock that ran just above the waterline, then a series of rapids, small waterfalls, drop-offs, and more ledges. The descent had become mountaineering rather than hiking. After a particularly precarious section, we took a breather.

"I'm glad we came this way," Brandon remarked. "It's awesome."

"Beautiful. Spectacular. Stunning," I agreed, a willing participant in ignoring our increasingly dire predicament as dimness foretold nightfall. In wet pants we were too cold to sit long. For a few minutes the going was easier until we came to a ledge just wide enough to support half the width of a foot. At its end loomed another large boulder, larger still than the one that had dammed the gorge above. It blocked our view and our way. Brandon worked his way along a crevice and under an overhang until he reached the boulder, which was higher than he was tall. He peered between the boulder and the side wall for what seemed like a long time while I waited some ten yards back, there not being space for both of us where he crouched. He finally looked back, not at me, but behind me. I followed his eyes as he retraced our route until his gaze returned locked on mine. "We're fucked," he said matter-of-factly.

Adrenalin surged in me. I made my way closer to him, leaning my weight into the rock wall for balance. I groped for an edge or crevice to use as a handhold, but found only blemish-free, water-polished rock. My feet ached and knees felt like moss as I balanced precariously behind him.

"Is there any good news?" I asked.

"There's a blind drop-off here. I can't see how far down it is." The massive boulder damming the gorge and blocking our descent had created a waterfall. Water poured over the top and around the sides in a way that prevented him from looking over and down without getting swept away in the surging current.

Brandon had been studying the formations around us while I was maneuvering close to him. "There's no way up and around that I can see, at least no safe way. We'd have to climb above the Tapeats, probably have to go all the way back to where we came down this morning."

I confirmed his assessment, adding: "That would make it completely dark long before we got back. Malcolm would be shitting bricks." It would be a tough call for our friend and traveling companion Malcolm Gray having to decide where, or even whether, to search for us in the dark. If he was sure we needed help, he would come for us as I would for him, without hesitation. But such certainty was impossible. Getting himself hurt would put us at greater risk if, ultimately, the real need was for someone to hike out for rescue. Three of us were potentially fucked in the canyon, not just two.

From my vantage point, clinging to the rock wall, unable to see past or get around Brandon, I couldn't add to his assessment. I could only observe that this would be our real descent into the abyss. Once we went over, there was no way back up if we couldn't reach Flint. We'd be trapped.

Though cold, tired, and tense, I felt quite clearheaded. Just to be sure, I undertook a conscientious clear-headedness examination to make certain I was thinking in a way that would not lead to self-recriminations later. Realizing at once that no such guarantee was possible assured me that my mind was still functioning. If Brandon should be seriously hurt, or worse, I would blame myself unmercifully the rest of my life. That awareness, and its accompanying terror, told me I was mentally alert. It was decision time.

Brandon regarded me calmly, waiting to hear what we'd do. "Don't look at me," I said with resolve. "You're in a better position to assess the situation than I am. You've laid out the alternatives clearly. I can't think of anything to add. We can go over or back up. I'm with you either way."

He looked above, around, and below, then back at me. His eyes told me he had no hesitation for himself. He had a look of calculated abandon I had seen earlier at the waterfall just before he jumped into the pool. I was the problem.

"I think we should go for it," he said hesitantly, indicating he was prepared for a contrary decision from me.

"Then go for it," I said with finality.

He started taking off his boots. I wanted to advise him to leave his boots on for protection, but it didn't strike me as a great time to say something parental. What, I asked myself, would I say to Malcolm in the same situation? I'd give him my best advice and he'd do whatever he thought best. I should treat Brandon with the same respect, I admonished myself. I have to figure out how we can discuss options without it becoming a father-son hierarchical thing. Brandon would want my best shot. It's all in how I say it.

Just as I resolved to speak, Brandon said, "I think it'll be better if I keep my boots on in case I hit something. They're already wet anyway. You'd probably better keep yours on too, at least until I yell back to you what I find. Let me give you my stuff and you can throw it over with yours once I'm down."

Before I could tell him how impressed I was with his judgment, he had turned, slipped into the current and was gone. I heard his splash. I willed myself to breathe, but couldn't. I strained to see over the falls. The top of his head came into view, then disappeared, then came back into view, bobbing up and down. Then he got far enough beyond the drop-off that I could see his whole head. He turned and looked back but I couldn't read his expression in the dim light. He started to swim on, then turned, treading water with difficulty because of the boots. "Throw me the stuff," he yelled at the top of his voice.

He retrieved what I threw and, treading water, waved me in. The current sucked me over, then under. I came up quickly, disoriented. I followed Brandon's shouts to the end of the pool, using all my energy to move the heavy weights on my feet. He reached out and helped me up on the rocky beach. I looked anxiously ahead to see if we had trapped ourselves between drop-offs. The dense vegetation and flat terrain told me we were down before I actually spotted the line of Flint Creek.

Brandon gazed back at the dammed gorge. "If we had come this way this morning, we wouldn't have made it to my waterfall."

I noticed with pleasure how he referred to it, but, still catching my breath, my heart still pounding out disaster scenarios in my head, I could only manage to nod my agreement. I wanted to say something meaningful or symbolic or at least memorable, but I couldn't speak. I just sat there drained. Brandon, meanwhile, matter-of-factly analyzed the consequences for our whole day if we hadn't decided in the morning to hike the Tonto instead of following Shinumo into

Merlin. Nor did he give me much time to ponder what thoughts I might render appropriate to the moment. He had been monitoring my breathing, noted it had returned to easy panting, reached for his hip pack, and commanded, "We'd better get going. It's almost dark. We've still got at least an hour ahead of us and we don't know what it will be like from here. You ready to truck?"

He was in charge and that was fine with me. "Lead on," I said. I had started to say, "Lead on, son." But it came out just, "Lead on."

Michael Quinn Patton is an independent organizational development and evaluation consultant. He was on the social sciences faculty of the University of Minnesota for eighteen years, including five years as Director of the Minnesota Center for Social Research. He is former President of the American Evaluation Association and author of Utilization-Focused Evaluation, *4th ed., and* Qualitative Research and Evaluation Methods, *3rd ed. He co-authored* Getting to Maybe: How the World Is Changed, *a book that applies complexity theory and systems thinking to innovation and developmental evaluation. His book* Grand Canyon Celebration: A Father-Son Journey of Discovery *was finalist for the 1999 Minnesota Book of the Year Award.*

Into the Woods

A dad and daughter navigate their way
through the Boundary Waters Wilderness.

FROM THE FIRST, KATE'S PACK HAD GIVEN US TROUBLE. It was one of mine. We'd tried it on at home, loaded with thirty pounds of gear, nearly half her own weight. It sagged on her shoulders, and the belt encircled her skinny waist like a ring around Saturn. Some angular part of the payload gouged her back. Even the short hike down to the end of the driveway and back seemed to stagger her.

So now, it is with some trepidation that my nine-year-old daughter steps from the canoe to begin the first portage of our three-day trip through northern Minnesota's canoe country wilderness. I want Kate to take part in portaging—carrying canoe and camping gear from lake to lake, a necessary ritual of traveling these waterways. At the same time, I want her to enjoy herself.

I've saved the heaviest items for my own pack, leaving Kate with soft, bulky gear that will rest more easily on her back. I hold her pack as she slides her thin arms into the straps.

"Stop and rest whenever you want," I say.

Then I watch her set out down the well-worn path. I

shoulder my own pack and the canoe and follow her into the dark shadows of the woods.

Kate has canoed with me since she was seven months old. She was a year and a half when we took our first long outing. Since then we have spent many days on the water, but never have we paddled and camped together in an area this remote. I don't doubt Kate will take to the paddling and camping. She'll even tolerate the mosquitoes.

No, my main concern is the portages, which range in length from a few feet to more than a mile. True, we could put in on a big lake, where islands and miles of water would give us plenty to explore without ever having to leave the lake. But I want to give Kate the true North Woods experience. And that means following the portage trails deep into the wilderness.

My worries evaporate once I reach the end of the portage. Kate stands smiling by the next lake, waiting for me to load her pack into the canoe. "I didn't get sore at all," she says brightly. "It was pretty easy." We load the canoe, Kate jumps into the bow seat, and we push off onto a long, island-studded lake rimmed by a rocky shore.

The two of us are traveling the Boundary Waters Canoe Area, a federal wilderness hard against the Canadian border. In bygone days, according to one explorer's map, it was called only "region of rocks and water."

It is these things and more. It is a land of 1.1 million acres of unbroken forest and some 2,500 lakes. It is a place where loons call and wolves howl. With few exceptions, it is a land where motors are not allowed and progress is measured by the firm bite of a paddle in clear water and the weight of a canoe and pack on your shoulders.

It is a natural place for kids, with freedom to hike, canoe, swim, fish, and explore, following the trails used by Ojibwa

Indians and French-Canadian voyageurs hundreds of years ago. The challenge is to get kids involved in the paddling, portaging, and routine chores of camping while keeping the trip easy enough—for parent and child—to be fun. That requires being prepared and knowing how to make adjustments in your plans.

After our portage, Kate and I face a long paddle across the lake. Here I know Kate will excel. She seems to love the feel of the paddle and the quiet glide of the hull through the water. We stop on an island for a quick lunch of pita bread, cheese, and sausage. I spread our map across my knees for Kate to see. We trace our route so far—down the light-blue fetch of Sawbill Lake, across the black dotted lines of our first portage and Alton Lake, to the red dot representing the island campsite where we now sit. After lunch, we make two more portages then pick a campsite on a rocky point that slopes into the lake. Kate leaps to the tasks at hand. She helps unload the canoe and carry gear up from shore. Together we pick a tent site, set the tent, and spread out sleeping pads and bags. As I start dinner, Kate forages for clusters of ripe blueberries. Low clouds settle in. Gray sky, gray water, hills of dark green spruce. The scene makes me ache with a melancholy I can't identify. I feel as though I sit on the cold, hard heart of the continent. The Ojibwa Indians saw spirits in every rock, wave, and tree. Floating on this lake with Kate, I feel the company of other spirits.

I first came to this country when I was twelve, on a canoe trip with my dad and younger brother. We'd paddled and portaged across several lakes before setting up camp, much as Kate and I have done. We spent the next three days canoeing, fishing, searching for turtles and beavers along the shore, hiking the portage trails, cooking and lounging about camp. "We could do the same thing," I tell Kate over breakfast. As I study the map, she munches a strawberry Pop-Tart, which is the perfect trail food: compact, packable, loaded with calories, hermetically sealed, and absolutely immune to spoilage. "We can stay on this lake and take short trips into other lakes today and tomorrow," I say. "We can swim and fish and paddle during the day and camp here at night. Or, we can do a loop."

A loop. Kate seems to come fully awake with this information. A loop! Why sit still when you can be on the move, ready to see something completely different. "Let's do a loop!" she says without hesitation.

I trace the route on the map: Northwest through a chain of a half-dozen lakes and scattered unnamed ponds and more than a dozen portages. Then east along something called the Louse River. From there, we'd puddle-jump through a knot of lakes, ponds, and portages back to our starting point. In all, about thirty-five miles and thirty-five portages, including a monster carry of one-and-a-half miles near the end. The problem is this: if we get tired halfway through, we have to finish the loop—or retrace our steps—to get home.

"It might be a lot of work," I say.

"Let's do it."

As the canoe glides toward the landing, I step into the shallow water with my rubber boots to protect the lightweight hull from rocks. I help Kate to shore, hold her pack, and watch as she disappears down the trail. I stow our two paddles and the spare in the stern of the canoe, secure them with a bungee cord, tuck the map in the pocket of the pack, and sling the pack onto my back. Then, making sure my footing is solid, I lift the canoe, cradle it overhead until it rests comfortably on my shoulders. Then I, too, set off down the path—no loose ends, nothing left behind. As much as anything in the Boundary Waters, I enjoy this efficiency of travel, the existential ease of moving through the country, like a salmon upriver or a vagabond on the highway. But what I remember most is the sight of Kate's blue back bouncing through the green woods, as her long, springy legs stride down the portage trail.

Clouds gather through the afternoon. A thunderstorm catches us on the portage to Malberg Lake. Drenched, we begin to search for a campsite. The first we find is second-rate, low, and marshy. The next several are taken by other canoeists. Finally, we paddle into a back bay just as another canoe emerges, occupied by three young men in rain gear. That can only mean that the site is already claimed, by them or someone else.

"Is that campsite taken?" I ask without much hope.

"Yeah, by a big black bear," one man says.

I laugh.

"We're not kidding."

I've run into bears many times in the Boundary Waters. They can be relentless in their quest for food. And they have always frightened me a bit. Too many *Outdoor Life* "true adventures" and tall tales from my dad.

"Let's go somewhere else," I say to Kate.

"Can we see the bear?" she asks.

Her curiosity and lack of fear surprise me. "O.K."

The site comes into view. No bear. Should we camp? Why not? These are black bears, not grizzlies, after all. For that matter, the bear could be headed toward any campsite on the lake by now. Besides, it's getting late.

We pitch the tent and spread our sleeping pads and bags inside. Then we paddle out into the lake to dip a big cooking pot for drinking water. When we turn the canoe toward shore, the bear stands on the broad outcrop, about a hundred feet from camp.

"Paddle hard," I tell Kate. We speed toward the bear and begin to yell. The bear runs off a few feet. It turns, sees that we're still coming, and flees into the brush. At the very least, I want the bear to think twice about coming back.

Dinner that night is pasta Parmesan—eaten as we look over our shoulders at the dark woods behind. We wash the dishes scrupulously and patrol the site for crumbs that would give the bear a reason to visit camp. We stash the garbage in a backpack with our food. Using a 100-foot length of strong rope, I suspend the pack between two widely spaced trees, a full fifteen feet off the ground. I stack the pots and pans by the fire grate. We build a fire. Thick smoke rolls from the wet wood, barely rising in the damp air.

Through the night I hear noises. Surely a mouse, I tell myself. Too noisy for a bear, which can pad through the forest with surprising stealth.

Suddenly the pots and pans scatter. I shout and think I hear the bear run off. Kate stirs groggily.

"Don't worry, honey, he's gone," I say.

The next day we strike camp and enter the Louse River. A portage appears where it doesn't belong. Is our map in error? Or am I? Have I simply lost track? Or worse, have we strayed off onto a different route? It's amazing how easily panic rises, how quickly you think of spending the night in the woods, location unknown, hacking out a makeshift camp in a stand of birch and balsam.

"Are we lost, Dad?"

"A little, but we'll find our way."

And so we do. After two portages, the Louse River gives way to a wide stretch of blue. It can only be Bug Lake. The name notwithstanding, it's a relief from the claustrophobia of what Kate and I have dubbed "the accursed Louse."

Portages here are gauged in rods, a logging measure that equals sixteen-and-a-half feet. The portage ahead measures 480 rods. Having walked down nearly three-dozen portage trails, I no longer have to run through the mathematics. No need to multiply by sixteen and divide by 5,280. As a unit of measurement, the rod has been thoroughly internalized. After three days I know how long it is, how it feels in the knees, in the thighs, along the neck where the pack straps and carrying yoke cramp your shoulders. Four hundred and eighty rods is exactly one-and-a-half miles.

By way of preparing Kate for this, I tell her we have the rest of the afternoon to take this portage, if necessary. We can rest as often as we want. She, in turn, regards the portage with bouts of giddy anticipation and melodramatic dread. "Oh, no!" she cries as we glide to the landing. "The portage!" But I can see she's smiling.

I help her with her pack. "If you get tired or if you're not sure of the way, just wait for me," I tell her. Then Kate, true to form, disappears down the trail before I can shoulder my load.

The trail rises from the lake, then levels. I try to turn my attention from the load on my back. I watch the forest floor for flowers, berries, and other small treasures. Suddenly, I come to a stretch of mud. Then another. Finally, a long black quagmire. No sign of Kate.

She has apparently found a way around. Or through. I take a step along the edge. Instantly, I sink to my knee. I try another step and hear a great sucking sound. It's my boot, buried deep in muck. I'm left standing on one leg like a giant flamingo, balancing precariously with only a sock on one foot and 100 pounds of pack and canoe on my back. I throw down my heavy load in disgust and dig through the mud in search of my boot.

I see Kate in the distance.

We return to the main path and portage on. The trail rises and travels along higher ground. Finally, it begins to drop, and I spot the refreshing blue of water through the dark trees. At water's edge, Kate has shed her pack and happily munches M&Ms and sunflower seeds. Her boots are caked with muck.

"What did you think?" I ask.

"Not bad."

We load and launch. As the canoe glides along, the little swamp river gradually widens and grows into a long, rocky lake. This place thrills me, and so does my daughter.

Greg Breining's stories and essays about travel and the outdoors have appeared in National Geographic Traveler, The New York Times, Audubon, Islands, *and other national publications. Among his many books are* Wild Shore: Exploring Lake Superior by Kayak, Super Volcano: The Ticking Time Bomb Beneath Yellowstone National Park, *and* A Hard-Water World: Ice Fishing and Why We Do It. Paddle North: Canoeing the Boundary Waters—Quetico Wilderness *will be published this fall by Minnesota Historical Society Press. He lives in St. Paul, Minnesota.*

* * *

We Should Have Stayed Home

The best laid plans of daredevil dads…

SAM DECIDES WE SHOULD SPEND A DAY AWAY FROM PHONES, chores, neighbors, TV, and the week before.

"Let's go exploring," he says. "Let's take the road less traveled."

It is Saturday night, and Sam has just started planning a family day for tomorrow. But everyone is happy, and I am happy that everyone is happy.

I think.

I set my alarm early so I can get things ready. Being prepared helps me get through each of Sam's adventures. I pack the cooler with lunch and water. I get dressed, make coffee, and feed the cats. I wake the kids, which doesn't require the usual coaxing. All I have to says is, "Day with Dad," and they are dressed and eating cereal when Sam strolls in, yawns his stretchy bearlike "it's my day off" yawn, and asks why we're all up so early.

It's on days like this that I most resemble my mother.

With a practiced glare and my teeth clenched, I remind Sam of the plans he made the previous evening. He shrugs his "so-shoot-me-I-forgot shrug" then gets dressed quickly, and I hand him his travel coffee mug as we load up the 4x4.

Once on the road, we pass the air-conditioned mall, movie theaters, restaurants, gas stations, and all other signs of civilization. Eventually, there are no more homes, businesses, cars, or trucks. The road is no longer paved; just the desert and the mountains surround us. My husband is now in Four-Wheel-Drive Heaven.

I am trying to be a good sport and see this as a family quest, but impending doom is all my intuition allows. I picture various forms of disaster even as I look out the passenger window and try to enjoy the beauty of Arizona's muted colors and unusual wildlife. My heart just isn't in it, and my enthusiasm is insincere.

At about noon, the kids announce they are hungry. Sam suggests a roadside picnic. But I know Sam. He sees a road and wants to go down it because his idea of "roadside" is as far off road as he can maneuver his truck. There is no extra thought, just, "How dangerous could it be? Live a little. Don't be like your mother." He uses that line for extra pressure and adds, "What do I have four-wheel-drive for if I can't use it?"

Sam pulls off the road and starts down a trail. Actually, it's not a trail. It's more like a very narrow path. Deeper and deeper we go, far from sight of the main road. I check my cell phone and, understandably, have no signal. I hold my breath and close my eyes.

Then Sam finds the perfect spot. It might be perfect because the road ends. Sam backs up into the side of the trail and just then, a swarm of bees attacks our 4x4. I barely suppress a rising wave of panic.

You see, we live in the Southwest, the newly adopted home of the Africanized k iller bees. Last week, an elderly man had a heart attack when he was mobbed by bees presumed to be Africanized killers. He died before the paramedics got there. They played a neighbor's call to 911 on the 5:00 news, the 5:30 news, the 6:00 news, the 10:30 news, and the 11:00 news. "They're swarming. They're stinging. He's down. They've killed him!" she screamed every half hour.

I wonder who will call 911 for us when the Africanized killer bees attack us. I can imagine the report on the 5:00 news, the 5:30 news, the 6:00 news, the 10:30 news, and the 11:00 news: "Attacking Africanized killer bees kill family of four. Wife's final words: 'I did not want to go!'"

I know enough about Africanized killer bees to know that the queen bee lays 3,000 eggs a day, and 3,000 eggs a day eventually become 3,000 aggressive stinging bees. Watching them bounce angrily against the window, I screech, "Sam, get us out of here!"

Sam goes forward, revving the motor, then he backs up away from the bees.

"Sam!"

He tries to move forward again, but the motor just groans.

Then, we begin slipping backwards.

At this point, I'm screaming. The kids are screaming. And, I swear, Sam yells at the top of his lungs, "*Far out!*"

So now we're stuck in a ditch. The bees are gone, but we've sunk into the earth.

After climbing out and examining the situation, Sam leaves me with the kids. "Have fun. Make a picnic out of it," he says as he hikes off to get help. He also says, "I don't know why you're always getting so pissed at me. It's not like I did this on purpose."

Four hours later Sam returns.

He has returned as a passenger in a flat bed monster truck

that widens the trail as it maneuvers its way to where we are. Sam and the driver are laughing as they pull up.

I, on the other hand, have been stuck with a broken 4x4 and two whining kids—kids who have said nothing but, "We could've stayed home and at least played Nintendo," and "There's nothing good to eat here."

We tried to picnic, but my sons didn't want chicken, apples, or chips. I brought Coke; they wanted Dr. Pepper. The only smile came when my five-year-old looked down at his feet and found bullet casings. Using my husband's favorite fitted Yankees hat as a container for collecting these muddied relics was my idea.

Of course, I obsessed to myself about the possible dangers we could encounter if Sam never got back. I thought about ax murderers, snakes, mountain lions, and, of course, the bees.

But here comes Cool Dad in this monster truck. The driver lets Sam help hook up the injured 4x4. Sam is happy. The kids get to sit in the cab of the monster truck. The kids are happy. Three hundred seventy-five dollars later, we're dropped off at our home. I'm not as happy as Sam and the kids.

We wind up eating McDonald's in our family room while the kids fight over Nintendo. The kids remember the day for various reasons: the bee swarm, the monster truck, the ditch, and the bullet casings. For some reason, maybe it is a male bonding thing, sliding into the ditch has become "Mom's fault" because I was afraid of bees. And to make the experience complete, Sam wants to trade in his 4x4 for a monster truck. He envisions this as a way to make cash on weekends "when others get stuck in ditches like we did."

He thinks this could happen to someone else.

Felice Prager is a freelance writer and multisensory educational thera-pist from Scottsdale, Arizona. Hundreds of her essays have been pub-lished locally, nationally, and internationally in print and online. She is the author of the recently released book, Quiz It: Arizona. *To find out more about Felice's book or to find links to more of her work, please visit www.QuizItAZ.com.*

ANA RASMUSSEN

* * *

Climbing Trees
with My Baby

*A middle-aged mom finds rejuvenation while climbing
a giant fir tree with her nearly grown son.*

I AM THE MOTHER OF SONS, TWO TEENAGE BOYS NEARLY
grown, each head and shoulders taller than I. Lean and muscled and oh so beautiful. They are confident, smart, and as
handsome as their father when I fell in love with him, both of
us young, in full flower. Lately I have been surprised to find
my sons' charms working on me, on the girl in me, like the
charms of their father so long ago. I lap up their sideways attention and scant praise like it's the best thing going, losing my
footing a little, my mom-ness, my years. Who are these cocky,
playful young lions running loose in my house, making me
blush and gush like I haven't since I was a teenager myself? I
am in love, all over again.

My older boy, six-foot-two at nineteen, drops by unex-
pectedly to ask if I'd like to climb a tree with him, an eighty-
foot fir deep in the forest that edges our town. "When?" I ask,
aware of the day's carefully laid plans bulleted neatly in my
datebook.

"How about right now?" he replies.

I say yes, of course, surprised to be asked, to be assumed capable of such a feat, my agenda falling away, forgotten before his invitation. This could well be the only tree-climbing date I get; I wouldn't miss it for anything. "Just let me change," I say, "and I'll be ready to go."

Pawing through the pile of clothes on my floor for the right pants, shoes, sweater appropriately comfortable, sturdy, warm, I am struck with a heightened awareness of my girlness. My son is permanently dressed in clothing well-suited to tree climbing while my wardrobe these days is typical of a modern working woman. Patience never his long suit, my son paces the living room while I quickly find something and throw it on. Within five minutes of his arrival we are off.

On the short drive we talk about this and that—school, vacation, friends, nothing of much import. I feel that I am of little interest to him but I am becoming accustomed to this status in the eyes of my sons and am easy with his indifference. After a brief silence he asks me how long it's been since I've climbed a tree. My mind reviews its collection of scaled trees, including the tallest one to date—a forty-foot, dying pine he and his brother climbed with me in celebration of my fortieth birthday. I sense the concern behind his question as he assesses my readiness for the challenge ahead, the measure of rust on my skills. In truth, I can't remember the last time, but not wanting to be found lacking, I stretch the bounds of absolute honesty and say, "Within the year I think, probably last April."

He chuckles and says, "Been a while, huh?"

And I nod, smiling sheepishly; while I do not know another forty-something woman who has been in more trees than I have, for my climbing son nine months is far too long to stay stuck to the ground.

Once we park he takes off at a brisk pace up the trail, his long young male legs covering ground so quickly that my shorter older female ones must nearly jog to keep up. He does not look back nor do I ask him to slow down. The lines of this adventure are being drawn and I must show that I am still worthy to play with the boys.

The trail winds through meadow and forest until stopping abruptly at a brown, needle-blanketed clearing surrounding the base of a gigantic tree.

"Is this it?" I ask, panting, gaping at this massive creature and its myriad branches thick as my torso spiraling up and up and up.

"Yup," he says. "You still want to climb it?"

Alluring, enormous, daunting, I do not want to say no. I cannot. But the lowest branch is at least fifteen feet off the ground and I don't see any possible way for me—or anyone else, for that matter—to make that first step.

"How do you get up there?" I ask, trying to keep discouragement out of my voice.

"Here, I'll show you," he says. And the boy who has always been equal parts monkey and mountain goat puts each hand around a small nub of bark, steps up onto another and, in the space of a few seconds, gracefully swings himself up to that impossibly out-of-reach first branch. Sitting easily astride it he looks down at me, grinning for the first time this afternoon.

"What do ya think?" he asks.

My crest of excitement plummets. I know without a doubt I cannot duplicate the spider's trick he has just performed. Had he truly thought me capable of such strength and agility? I am sorry to disappoint him, though flattered again that he would have even considered it. He waits up there while I assess what really needs no assessing and then I tell him there's no way I can do that.

"Then I'll come down and help you find another way up, O.K.?"

And before I answer he is swinging down from the branch, confident as a cat, freefalling through the air to land lightly on his feet, ready to help his still-worthy mother.

He points to where a piece of wood I hadn't noticed before leans casually against the trunk. Some eight inches across, about five feet long, nearly stripped of bark, a few broken off branches stick out from its sides, none longer than six inches nor bigger around than my wrist.

"You could climb up that," he says.

I am incredulous at the suggestion but sense it is my only chance. I have become firmly attached to the idea of climbing this beautiful tree with my beautiful son. I walk over for a closer look but don't see much to inspire confidence.

"Won't it just slip out from under me when I put my weight on it?" I ask.

"Well," he says, pushing on it with both hands, "it looks pretty stable to me."

"O.K.," I say, not at all sure it will hold. "I'll give it a try. Would you keep it steady for me?" I ask, swallowing my life-long do-it-myself tomboy pride in one easy gulp.

"Sure," he says, as he leans into the branch.

And up I go, feet and hands finding just enough purchase along the broken branch, beyond it to the tree's bark, then upward on tiny unforeseen protrusions until I, too, reach that first impossible branch and haul myself up onto it in surprised triumph.

"You O.K.?" he calls up.

"Great," I say, smiling down at him.

He scrambles up for the second time and we begin our ascent. There are a plethora of branches. So many climbable routes present themselves, the choice of which branch when—a delectable, body-focused puzzle to figure out again and again. Each new move is considered, tested, taken—or rejected—sometimes briefly, at other times with more concentrated attention. I am climbing easily, smoothly, pleased with myself for being able to do what I am doing. My son climbs below or alongside me, his open face watchful of the choices I make. On his own, I know, he would be at the top by now but I sense no impatience in him. This climb is for me, for us together; it is a gift he has given us and I am welcome to receive it in whatever way I can.

"This is fun," I say. "Really fun. I love climbing trees. Why don't I do this more often?"

"Yeah," he says, "it's pretty cool, huh? But you gotta make sure you stay focused."

Advice well-timed, I realize, as I notice my blood racing as if I'd just had a double espresso. I wonder at the rush, sensing it is more than the excitement of the climb itself, even with its substantial physical challenges and the reliability of the firm ground moving farther and farther away. Then it hits me: it is the thrill of being up here with this young man, solicitous and concerned, watching my every move. In fact, I am giddy as a schoolgirl on a first date with a boy she really likes. He chose me. He's climbing a tree with me. He's paying attention to me. My cheeks pinken with this wildly unexpected realization, and I stop climbing for a moment to steady myself and slow my rapid pulse. Though I come close to chastising myself for the inappropriateness of my feelings, I decide against it. We have stumbled onto a sweet, surprising moment in our long, often tumultuous, always complex relationship. A moment to cherish, to be grateful for, to enjoy.

"You O.K., Mom?" he asks, his voice and face soft, easy, calming.

"Yeah," I say, "just finding my focus."

He watches me start up again, slower, more attentive to the tree on whose solid strength my life depends. "It's great you know how to climb trees so well," he says.

"What do you mean?" I ask, my ears pricked to this rare, offhand compliment.

"You know how to use your knees and elbows too, not just your hands and feet. A lot of people don't realize they're some of the best tools for climbing trees, but you do. That's cool."

This is high praise from a boy for whom climbing is a basic requirement in a life well lived. I don't know when I have felt so minutely seen, so specifically appreciated, and I am pleased with the impact of it. Blushing again, well above his head, my delight remains a secret held between me and this glorious tree.

The trunk's diameter shrinks dramatically the last twenty feet or so. When I question its ability to hold us safely so near the top he shows me a place where several branches come together to form a comfortable seat and says some people claim that as their zenith. I try it out but I'm in for the whole climb and turn to face the final, scary ascent. I tell him I'd better be quiet for a while so I can focus and he says that sounds like a good idea.

In a few moments our heads break through the uppermost canopy into the full sunshine of this perfect mid-December afternoon.

"Wow," I say, the vast expanse of the Monterey Bay stretching out before us, white foam of breaking waves delineating the union of land and sea. "Amazing."

I feel slightly woozy looking down at the ground eighty feet below so I keep my vision high, out over the treetops. I am in a state of exhilaration. It is hard for me to let it in, to believe I am really sitting with my firstborn at the top of this tall, tall tree at the summit of a long hill, high above our little town by the bay. I have to remember to breathe, to keep myself present, to feel the so slight breeze gently swaying my thin-limbed perch.

The scent of my son mingles with the fragrant fir, fresh sweat under his ripe t-shirt, both he and it a few days this side of a wash. A young man's smell. Lanky legs crisscrossed on the tiniest of platforms where the trunk forks into the two topmost branches, arms folded beneath his head, he leans back on a green, cone-studded bough and closes his eyes, smiling in the warm light of the sun. A lone monarch slowly circles us then floats lazily along its treetop way. Just seeing the ease of boy and butterfly encourages me to loosen my grip a notch, to relax a little more into the arms of this majestic tree, to delight in the incredible gift of this day.

"Thank you for bringing me up here, sweetie," I say, reaching out to touch his hand. "This is the best Christmas present I've had in a long, long time."

Turning slightly, he meets my gaze. "I'm glad you're here, mama," he says.

There we rest, together in the heart of a perfect peace.

Ana Rasmussen's two sons having flown so confidently, so beautifully into lives of their own making, she now has the freedom to follow her own heart. She will soon leave her career as a school counselor to work in sustainable agriculture, both as a farmer and as an advocate for food justice.

JENNIFER BOVÉ

✭ ✭ ✭

Den Mother

*Like a pack of coyotes, a family of five
heads off on a hunt.*

SOON AFTER WE STAKE OUT A CAMP IN EASTERN WASHINGTON'S
Colockum Wildlife Area, Chris starts laying down the law:
"Step lightly and stick close to me. No running, whining, or
fighting. And if you have to pee, do it now."

His voice is stern, but his finger wags playfully. The girls
gaze up at him with eyes open wider than their ears.

"Daddy, I feel a prickly in my shoe," announces Sophia, age
three.

Chris rubs his forehead. "Again?"

He kneels down to inspect her sock, and Rita, five, sighs
dramatically. "Aren't we ever gonna go?"

I duck into our camp trailer so nobody sees me giggling. I
wouldn't dare undermine the gravity of their mission—it's late
afternoon the opening day of archery elk season, and they
mean business. They discuss their plan of action and quibble
over who gets to use which call as Chris tucks every last lock
of golden hair into their camouflage hoods. As if on cue, both
girls buckle down and get serious, like wee warriors ready for
battle, and they study Chris with intent curiosity as he dusts
his beard with odor-absorbing baking soda. When everybody's

ready, they holler goodbye to me and toddle off into the woods, biting back all those words that want to spill out about the woodpecker sound and the fungus that might be poisonous and I need to pee now and when are we going to see some elk and can I squeeze the Hoochie Mama call yet?

The hunt is on.

This elk season, I'm wearing no camouflage except for a ball cap to hold back my hair. I probably won't stumble out of bed before light or drag into camp after dark with stories of big bulls that blew my cover. For the third year running, my family and I are roughing out a tradition of elk hunting in which I've assumed the role of scout, wrangler, camp cookie—den mother. I've waited anxiously, watching the edges of leaves turn russet and gold, for this two-week opportunity to escape to the woods together. Here, we can allow our kids the grace of wild living and nurture their love of the outdoors. Chris and I hope that by immersing them in September's rituals we're instilling a profound respect for the harvest that brings meat to our table.

Making things a bit more interesting this year, our kid clan has grown to include our six-week-old son Samson. I have never camped with a child quite so young, but based on previous experience, I imagine the simplicities of toting around a cute little cocklebur only will be matched by the moments migraines are made of.

On our first attempt at a family hunting trip two years ago, we camped in familiar country near Trout Lake, Washington; but it felt like uncharted territory with kids in tow. Take a couple of overprotective, hyper-hygienic parents with two toddlers, dump them in the dirty outdoors, and you're bound to require an adjustment period.

Every inch of our isolated campsite was powdered with

dust. Rain hadn't made it over the mountains in months, and the only creek in the area was closed to camping. Chris and I cringed when we turned our little ones loose from the safety of their car seats. Not only did they promptly sit right down on the ground without a care as to how much grit got into their shorts, but then they found sticks with which they could stir up a blizzard of dust. Didn't they consider itchy eyelids, black boogers or crusty butt cracks? Had they no concern for the sanctity of the sheets we all had to share?

"This is vegetable soup!" Rita beamed, teeth already rimmed in grime, as she added bits of grass and pine needles to her pothole.

Sophie tossed in a handful of sun-baked elk poop. "Tatoes!"

It took me about thirty-six hours of relentless nagging, trying to keep the girls clean, before I gave up exhausted. They were dirty, yes. Blotches of pine sap had glued crud to their hands, and twigs poked from tangled clumps of their hair. But they weren't puking or feverish or missing any limbs. They were alive, really alive. And it suddenly made sense that there was no better time or place to let them go wild.

When Chris and the girls leave me at the trailer, I hardly know what to do with myself. I could read or write, take nap or a hike, but with Sam asleep I figure I should probably go ahead and unpack. Funny how motherhood has skewed my sense of duty—maintaining domestic order sometimes seems easier than cracking open a good book.

Of course, like last year and the year before, I had every intention to pack lightly, bring just the essentials. And yet I was amazed all over again when I saw the mounds of family camping gear sprawling across the living room floor. There were the bulky basics, like the bow case, sleeping bags, tarp, coolers, food, diapers, water jugs, toilet paper, lantern, propane cylinders, and the catch-all camp box of smaller sundry necessities. Add to that additional items that may seem frivolous to the rugged and childless, but to a parent are almost indispensable: inflatable air mattress, pillows, extra blankets, collapsible camp chairs, enough spare shoes and clothes and jackets to split the seams of a lawn-size garbage bag, plus story books, stuffed animals, locally roasted organic coffee, and cream to go with it.

Rooting through the piles, I now begin questioning my compulsion to bring everything "just in case." Worse yet is knowing that even though it feels like I brought the kitchen sink, I will soon discover a semi-critical something we forgot that will trip us up when we least expect it. That first year at our Trout Lake camp, for example, it was peanut butter.

I was cooking dinner one evening, feeling perhaps a bit too smug about mastering the art of wild mothering, when Sophia began to shriek at the top of her lungs. I whipped around, hurling the spatula into the air, and gasped, "Hornet? Bear? What? What is it?"

"More pee-butter!"

My fair flower child had bailed into a shrill fit of tears because the one and only peanut butter jar I'd brought was empty.

Rita clamped her hands over her ears and rocked back and forth in her chair like an asylum patient. I took a deep breath and surveyed the dusky woods around me. Chris wasn't back from the day's hunt yet, so I was likely the only adult human within earshot, and all I could think as I looked at my screaming urchin smeared in peanut butter and granola was bear bait. Could there be any better attractant? I wanted to clamp my hand over her messy little mouth or bribe her with chocolate or just give up and go home, but I knew none of it would work out in the long run. So calmly clenching my teeth, I turned off the Coleman stove, planted Sophie in her kid carrier, roused Rita, and set off down the trail behind camp.

"Where are we going?" Rita asked.

Where wasn't the point; we were just going.

Sophie was curious enough to calm down, licking her fingers and patting me on the head. "Where's Daddy?"

"Hush, girls, and maybe we'll hear an elk."

We walked till we found a good clear spot to sit down and listen. The woods were velvety quiet except for the elkish mew of a Northern flicker.

"Elk cow!" Rita croaked in a loud stage whisper.

I shook my head and flapped my hands like wings, hoping to inspire mute communication.

Sophie, already sick of sitting still, didn't take the hint. "Bunny!" she squealed, pointing down the trail.

"Sophie, shhhhh!" Rita hissed. "Oh, it is a bunny. Look, Mom!"

I frowned and pressed a finger against my lips.

"Well," Rita sighed, "can I have that red rock?"

I shook my head hard, finger still glued to my face.

"But it's red. Red is my favorite color."

I was about to abandon the expedition when a faint whistle wound its way through the trees, followed by a series of hoarse chuckles.

"Elk!" Sophie gasped.

I nodded, my own heart fluttering.

"It's a bull elk," Rita informed us. "He's bugling."

Again, the bull squealed. He wasn't close, but near enough to give us a thrill.

"Do you think Dad sees him?" Rita asked.

I shrugged.

Both girls raised their eyebrows and shrugged back without saying a word, and I couldn't help but smile.

Shadows shift across camp, and I feel the woods pulling at some instinct deep in my core. Our gear is pretty much unloaded, or at least strewn about enough to make room for eating and sleeping, and the urge to slip away is too strong to resist. I bundle up Sam just as he starts to stir, securing him in a wrap against my chest. Jake and Buddy perk up their ears and beg me with big brown eyes to come too. Wandering this country with a child—particularly a newborn—makes me feel vulnerable in a way I never did before I had kids, and the dogs give me a sense of security. So I slap my thigh and we set off down the road, giving a wide berth to the area where Chris has taken the girls, and I swell with the freedom of this simple act. For once I don't have to breathe a word. I can just walk with my quiet companions and watch the evening fall while I wonder what the rest of our family is up to right now.

I've tagged along on enough of their hunting excursions to know that sometimes, like on a no-nap day, the girls are apt to whisper and squirm or dawdle over flowers along the way, and everybody gets frustrated with the push and pull until we agree it's best to ditch the hard-core hunt and simply enjoy being outside. But other times, our girls are truly on their game, and they thrive on the intensity of the goal.

While we were scouting the Colockum before the season started, we built a few blinds, hefting branches into haphazard piles that became fortresses where a kid could wiggle and dig in the dirt without being seen. After we finished the last one, we decided to hunker down in it and call to see if any elk would answer, practicing for the upcoming hunt. Chris let the girls belt out a couple of very convincing mews with their own perfectly pitched voices, then he motioned for Rita to blow the Cow Girl call, and Sophie worked the Hoochie Mama so well that they sounded like a small herd of restless cows. Before they got too carried away, though, Chris issued the "cut" signal. We all held our breath to listen. This is the one time I remember everything happening the way expert elk caller Jim Horn says it should. To our amazement, we heard a bull answer just a few hundred yards off in the deep timber. Chris blew his bugle, hoping to incite the territorial instinct that would draw the bull in to investigate an intruder. Within moments, that bull was no more than a hundred yards from us, hidden by a thick stand of young firs, scrabbling his antlers in the brush and bellyaching up a storm. We were all grinning and giving thumbs up signs when he spooked and crashed away, never offering us a glimpse. But the girls had seen elk before, so they understood the magnitude of the beast we'd called in. They felt the power of his presence, the primal rush that reminds us how deeply our roots twine with the wild, and it sparked eagerness in them to get out hunting with Dad.

As much as I treasure these times with my family, I'd be lying if I didn't tell you that I itch to hunt too every time Chris rouses before light and sneaks away. What I ache for is suiting up and creeping through the woods, crouching motionless in musky loam for hours, becoming part of the wilderness in a deep and secret way that only a hunter knows. Throughout bow season, I dream of elk more than any other time of year. I hunt them and ride them, touch their antlers, even spar with them as if I were an elk myself. And, in the dim gray light of morning, I lie awake listening to Chris's footsteps crunch away from me and our tender sleeping babes, and I try to travel with him in my mind. I know the ground, the smells. I try to will the animals to my husband. Often, I'm sure I can feel the arrow leave his bow, certain it has met with warm hide. But then Chris comes back with bloodless hands, and I realize I was dreaming. Some mornings, though, the dream proves true.

Last year, just as sun was coaxing the girls from sleep, Chris returned to camp hollering. I was already up with coffee and turned to see what the ruckus was about.

"I got one," he breathed. "We gotta get her out before it gets hot."

My gut cinched up and I started whirling through camp, taking stock of what we needed and feeling immensely unprepared. I spurred the kids, shouldered Sophie in the pack, and stuffed energy bars in their hands for breakfast. Rita offered to carry the rope we'd need to rig up a sling for packing out quarters. Though I knew the mile hike to the elk was going to be tiresome enough for a four-year-old, not to mention subsequent trips in and out with meat, I didn't doubt her resolve and let her lug the rope as long as she wanted to.

When we reached the shoulders Chris had already removed from the downed cow, Rita touched the smooth brown fur with awe. The rest of the elk was too far into thick brush for the girls to reach, so Rita marveled at the pieces she could see, the very mortality of the flesh that would feed us. She wanted to see the blood, to touch a bone. I could tell she was gleaning something significant about life and death. I'd already turned Sophie loose from the pack so Chris could use it to haul out a hind leg, and she stood close beside Rita but didn't touch the hide. She wasn't quite as taken with the gravity of it all, but she watched her older sister's expressions intently.

"Look at this beautiful meat, Sophie," Rita mused.

"Yeah," Soph said. "That's meat."

Chris trudged back out of the brush, grunting under the weight of one massive hindquarter in the kid pack.

Rita looked at him and said, "Dad, it is good you killed an elk."

Tonight, I hike to the top of a dry grassy ridge and watch the sun burn down to red embers along the western horizon, lungs tight and exhilarated in the cool air. Night is brewing. Animals are on the move. I hear them. A gentle thunder trembles through the forest on the far side of the small valley. Heart quivering, I squat down to shrink my silhouette and growl at the dogs to keep still. All of a sudden, a river of elk bursts from the trees, pounding earth and pouring toward me and my tiny son. I snatch Jake's bristled scruff to restrain the irrepressible impulse hardwired in his heeler brain. As the elk break to the south, I spy a bull among the herd, carrying his branched antlers like a crown. Somebody riled this herd into a full run, and I have a hunch who it is.

Just after the elk spill over a hill and out of sight, three camouflaged figures step into the twilit valley—two of them markedly shorter than the third. I wrap my arms around Samson to steady him. Then the dogs and I trot down the slope to our brood, and we meet up like a pack of coyotes. I cup the little red cheeks that come rushing to me, kiss smiling mouths whose tongues are wagging all sorts of exciting news in breathless bursts. Chris slings an arm around me, pulls me in. He didn't get a chance to shoot, but they got to see the elk right up close. He says I should come along tomorrow evening. He'll hunt serious in the morning, but he wants us to experience some of this together, even if Sam's fussing might compromise his chance at a kill. I clasp Rita's ice-cold hand in mine, realizing I should share some of the action with my girls, show them Mom's still got some grit. Chris hoists Sophie over his shoulder, and we head back to camp for dinner.

The season guarantees at least a few surprises—only a fool would traipse off into the woods with three youngsters believing everything is under control. Among the things I can expect are bickering, homesickness, and potty problems at inopportune moments. Hikes that are too short for me will seem miles too long for the kids. We are guaranteed some serious shortage of spoons or socks, and somebody will get scared of noises in the night. But the thrill of leaving civilization behind is brimming in each of us. In so many ways, this wilderness is where we feel most at home. And so if we're lucky, we'll also be blessed with pockets full of pebbles and pine cones, coyote lullabies, one elk to take home, and the absolute wonder of it all.

Jennifer Bové also contributed "A Place Among Elk" to this collection.

Resources for Outdoor Families

Gear Up to Get Outside:

A Happy Camper: www.ahappycamper.com

First Treks, Outdoor Gear for Kids and Active Families: www.firsttreks.com

Family Camping Gear: www.familycampinggear.com

Backcountry Food:

MaryJanesFarm Outpost: Easy gourmet organic food for back country travelers, www.backcountryfood.org

Tips, Tales, and Travel Destinations for Families:

Take a Child Outside: A comprehensive web site of resources, including a searchable database of nationwide outdoor activities and opportunities to share your adventure stories, www.takeachildoutside.org

Travel For Kids: A family travel guide for planning vacation trips with children as fun adventures, www.travelforkids.com

Family Travel Network: The definitive where, why and how site for family travelers, www.familytravelnetwork.com

REI Family Adventures: Features special versions of tried-and-true REI adventures, with added features

catered to the entire family,
www.rei.com/adventures/activity/family.html

National Wildlife Federation Green Hour Program: Lots
of good info on the benefits of getting kids outdoors,
www.greenhour.org

Books for Backcountry Parents:

*Extreme Kids: How to Connect with Your Children Through
Today's Extreme (and Not So Extreme) Outdoor Sports* by
Scott Graham, Wilderness Press, 2006.

The Kids Campfire Book: Official Book of Campfire Fun by
Jane Drake and Ann Love, Kids Can Press, Ltd., 1998.

Kids in the Wild: A Family Guide to Outdoor Recreation by
Cindy Ross and Todd Gladfelter, Mountaineer Books,
1995.

Kid's Survival Handbook by Claire Llewellyn, Tangerine
Press, 2002.

*Last Child in the Woods: Saving Our Children from Nature-
Deficit Disorder* by Richard Louv, Algonquin Books,
2005.

MaryJane's Outpost: Unleashing Your Inner Wild by
MaryJane Butters, Clarkson Potter, 2008.

*The Outdoor Family Fun Guide: A Complete Camping,
Hiking, Canoeing, Nature Watching, Mountain Biking,
Skiing, Climbing, and General Fun Book for Kids (and
Their Parents)* by Michael and Nicole Hodgson,
McGraw-Hill, 1998.

Parents' Guide to Hiking & Camping: A Trailside Guide by
Alice Cary, W. W. Norton & Company, 1997.

Acknowledgments

Wild with Child was a collaborative project, and I'm so thankful to the contributors for breathing life into it.

I have years' worth of appreciation and respect for Jan Brocci, Managing Editor of the Rocky Mountain Elk Foundation's *Bugle* magazine. Jan has published my writing, improved my skills with straightforward and thoughtful editing, and helped me track down authors and stories for my collections. The Rocky Mountain Elk Foundation is an outstanding organization dedicated to preserving wild habitat in North America. Check out their efforts at www.rmef.org.

Thanks, too, to Katie McKalip at Outdoor Writers Association of America (www.owaa.org) and Jen Leo (www.jenleo.com) for putting the word out and helping me find incredible writers. Of course, I'm ultimately and infinitely thankful to James O'Reilly, Larry Habegger, Christy Quinto, and Susan Brady of Travelers' Tales/Solas House for bringing this book to fruition.

Big hugs go out to all of my family near and far whose love and support give me strength to face the world.

And, finally, I thank my husband Chris and our three kids, each of whom was wondrously wild from the get-go. Rita was brought by the cranes, Sophie ripened under a wild prairie sun, and Sam was very nearly born in a berry patch. These amazing people are the foundation of everything I do. They put up with the hours I spend at the computer, and when I've been sitting around too long, they drag me outside where I remember that inspiration cannot survive without real adventures in life and love.

"Foreword: Into the Wild" by Mark Jenkins published with permission from the author. Copyright © 2010 by Mark Jenkins.

"Uphill Infinity and the Chocolate Chip Cookies" by Betsy Kepes published with permission from the author. Copyright © 2010 by Betsy Kepes.

"The Tender Groin of the Land" by Fred Bahnson first appeared in volume 31, issue 3 of *Pilgrimage Magazine* in November 2006. Published with permission from the author. Copyright © 2006 by Fred Bahnson.

"The Snowcave" by Mark Jenkins published with permission from the author. Copyright © 2010 by Mark Jenkins.

"Bobble Your Stopper and Wiggle Your Piminnow" by Jim Spencer published with permission from the author. Copyright © 2010 by Jim Spencer.

"A Place Among Elk" by Jennifer Bové first appeared in *Heart Shots: Women Write About Hunting*, edited by Mary Zeiss Stange, in 2003. Reprinted with permission from the author. Copyright © 2003 by Jennifer Bové.

"The Facts of Life" by Lily Dayton published with permission from the author. Copyright © 2010 by Lily Dayton.

"Migration" by Leslie Leyland Fields published with permission from the author. Copyright © 2010 by Leslie Leyland Fields.

"The Gift of Artemis" by Durga Yael Bernhard first appeared in *Heart Shots: Women Write About Hunting*, edited by Mary Zeiss Stange, in 2003. Published with permission from the author. Copyright © 2003 by Durga Yael Bernhard.

"We'll Do Whitney, Right?" by Bernadette Murphy first appeared in the *Los Angeles Times* in October 2005. Reprinted with permission from the author. Copyright © 2005 by Bernadette Murphy.

About the Editor

Jennifer Bové set out into the uncharted territory of motherhood nine years ago and has since covered a lot of ground with her family of five. They've moved cross-country three times, always finding their way to wild places. Whether they are elk hunting, berry picking, or splashing in a secret swimming hole somewhere, the Bové clan thrives on outdoor adventure.

When she's indoors, Jennifer writes for *MaryJanesFarm* magazine (www.maryjanes-farm.org) and is an award-winning contributor to *Your Big Backyard* (www.nwf.org). She is the editor of two other anthologies, *The Back Road to Crazy* and *A Mile in Her Boots*.

After living in the wilds of Washington, Montana, and Missouri, this former field biologist and her family have nestled into a remarkably remote expanse of woods near Calico Rock, Arkansas.

Stop by for a visit at www.bovesboots.blogspot.com.